LAKEVIEW MEMORIES

Growing up in Lakeview in the 1920s, 30s & 40s

Written by
MURIEL B. MACHAUER

LAKEVIEW MEMORIES

Copyright © 2015 by Muriel MacHauer

Cover by: Parajunkee Design

All rights reserved. No part of this book may be reproduced in any form by any electronic or mechanical means including photocopying, recording, or information storage and retrieval without permission in writing from the author.

ISBN-13: 978-0996176101
ISBN-10: 0996176101

Contact the author at:
Email: mbmachauer@gmail.com

Printed in the U.S.A

*This is dedicated to my daughter, Bonnie MacHauer Herberger.
You are always there in everything I do.*

Table of Contents

Part I	Introduction	1
Part II	Childhood Memories	3
	Michael J. Artall	10
	Frances "Honey" Virgadamo Blondo	11
	Merlin Bonie	14
	Walter C. Bonie	16
	Thomas Casey	20
	The Connick Family	23
	Lois Junod Dahlman	29
	Albert J. Derbes	33
	Rosemary Mccoy Baudier Favalora	38
	Adele Yost Foucheau	44
	Patricia Howell Frost	47
	Valerie Fitzgerald Gaffney	49
	David Henry MacHauer	53
	Muriel Bonie MacHauer	57
	Betty Witcher McMahon	69
	Audrey Schwartzenburg Maduell	72
	Louis Marion Maduell	79
	Joyce Keiffer Mohr	84
	Ora Dedebant Mollere	86
	Connie Hinkel Negrotto	88
	Armand Peyroux	92
	Marie Virgadamo Porrovechio	95
	Pat Reilly Rebenne	97
	Gerri Quaid Rodrique	99
	Robert Roesler	101
	Sister Angele Marie Sadlier, O'carm	104
	Josephine Cartazzo Santora	113
	Rosemary Spies Schwartz	116

	Robert E. Smith	118
	Claude Spies	121
	Sue Spilsbury	125
	Mary Skelly Stumph	130
	Mary Meek Swanson	132
	Lena Bacino Turpin	135
	Richard Villarubia	139
Part III	Images of Lakeview	141
	Conclusion	165
	Acknowledgements	166
	Credits	167

PART I
INTRODUCTION

My purpose in producing this small book is to gather and share the stories of Lakeview, a suburb of New Orleans, Louisiana. This is a unique community, wrestled from swampland on the southern shores of Lake Pontchartrain in the early 20th century. It is still part of New Orleans and their histories are intertwined. I am personally connected in one way or another to the places, people and, events, both good and bad, described in these stories.

My focus is on the people who originally settled here after the land reclamation efforts were started and considered successful. The original founder of New Orleans, Jean-Baptiste Le Moyne de Bienville, chose this area of the Mississippi River because of the already established trading post and fort on Bayou St. John. Bayou St. John linked Lake Pontchartrain to the river and the river bank was considered relatively high ground. Bayou St John was initially considered the eastern edge of the area to be reclaimed for Lakeview. In the early days of New Orleans it was only swampland, the northern edge of the city was considered City Park Avenue. When Lakeview was set for reclamation City Park Avenue was the southern edge. Where Lakeview sits now was a cypress swamp only useful for grazing cattle, but too prone to flooding to warrant permanent settlement. In the 1830s, the New Basin Canal was cut through from the lake to the center of New Orleans to be used as a shipping canal. After the development of the canal, a resort was built in the lakeshore area around present-day West End and later developed into a hotel, restaurant and amusement park. But, it wasn't until the early 20th century that the land around West End became inhabited. The New Basin Canal was still in use when Lakeview was developed and the two adjoining service roads that ran on either side of the canal, served as the western edge of Lakeview until the canal was filled in and became West End Blvd and Pontchartrain Blvd. The New Basin Canal is mentioned in these stories consistently, it was a fun swimming resource for many Lakeview children and it's iconic Black Bridge and boat traffic stands out in most of our memories.

In the early days of Lakeview commercial centers of activity on the lake was limited to three areas. The first was the West End area where a lighthouse, hotel, restaurant with a bar and dance floor, pavilion, and the Southern Yacht Club were located. The second area was located in the Bayou Saint-Jean area. This was where the French built a fort and the Spanish later named it to Bayou St. John, the locals calling it simply, Spanish Fort. The third area was Milneburg where Elysian Fields Ave and the Pontchartrain railroad ended at the lake. The railroad was well known as The Smoky Mary" to locals. In the Milneburg area, there was also a lighthouse, along with a lovely beach and large oak trees that crept down to the water's edge. The old lighthouse still stands on the University of New Orleans campus.

In 1887, there was an attorney by the name of Charles Louque who made a study of dykes, dams, and drainage methods. He also studied the swamp land between Bayou St. John and the New Basin Canal. He and a few others formed a company called the New Orleans Reclamation Company with initial capital of $50,000 and 2,615 acres of the area, which would later become Lakeview, were acquired. The company's name was later changed to The New Orleans Land Company. To help things along, the New Orleans

▼ Map of Lakeview circa 1926, after reclamation had started, Lakeview Map, recreation. Courtesy of Rachel Rivera

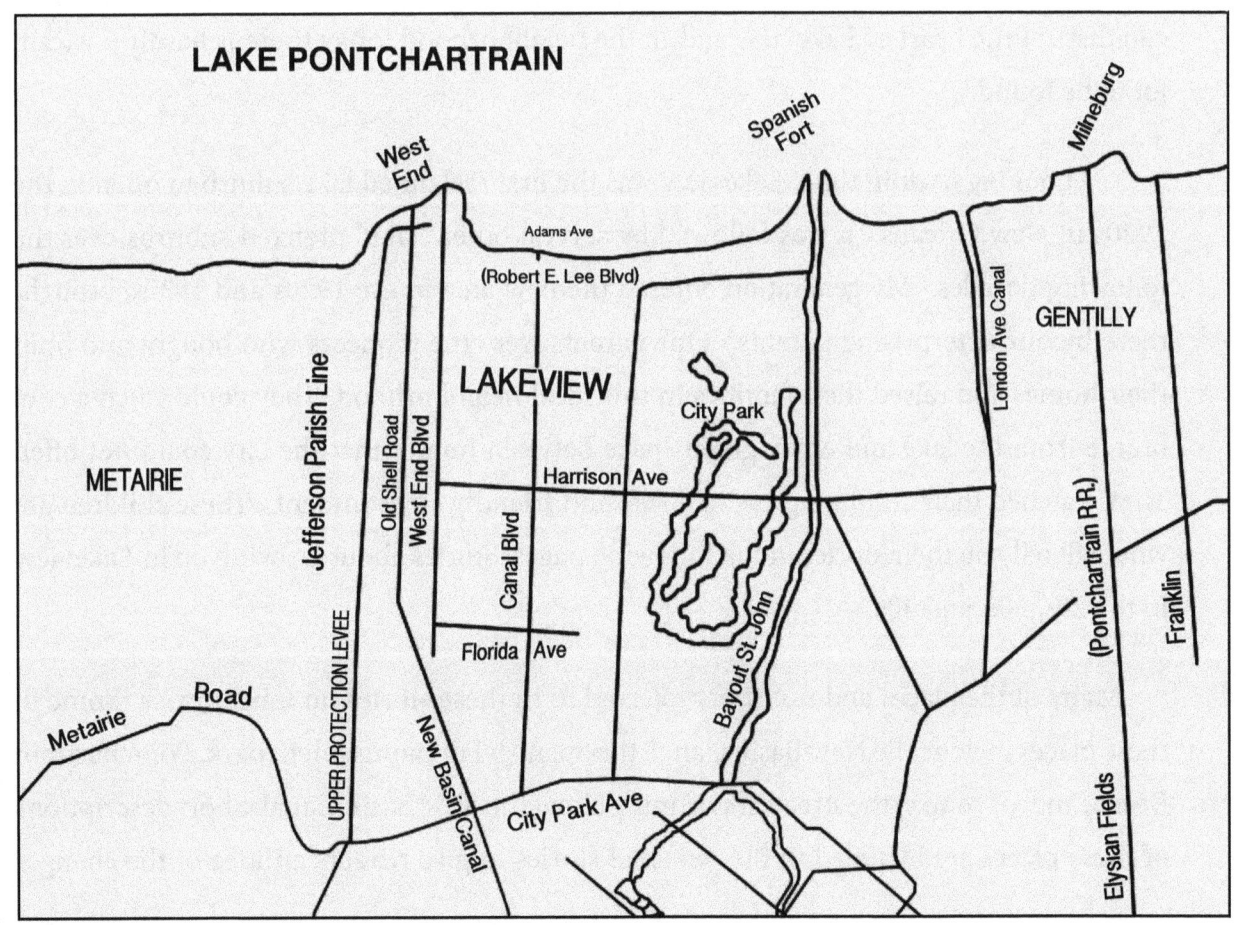

Sewerage and Water Board built pumping station #6 in 1896 on the parish line canal, what is now known as the 17th Street Canal. Three years later, pumping station #7 was built on the Orleans Canal near present day Florida Avenue. To drain the area, the New Orleans Land Company began dredging canals in Lakeview, connecting the canals to these pumping stations. By 1905, the swamp began to drain and lots could be sold, thereby, making the company the largest real estate business in the city.

Among the first realtors to advertize and sell lots were George Deninger, Albert J. Derbes, A.K. Roy, John Stafford and Robert E. Smith. By 1908, the first homes were built on West End Boulevard, which at the time, was the service road along the New Basin Canal. A significant growth took pace in the 1920s. Buyer confidence was promoted by the improved flood control plans initiated by the newly created Orleans Levee Board. By 1929, the Great Depression was in full swing and lot sales ground to a halt. Many of the lots of Lakeview were unoccupied and overgrown with weeds. It took until after WWII ended to jump-start lot sales again. Sales increased greatly and have continued at a startling rate to this day, making Lakeview an enviable zip code to reside within. Not even a broken levee can disrupt the heart of Lakeview and in the neighborhood today there is hardly a vacant lot to be found.

Looking back in time, Lakeview was the first reclaimed lake suburb to open in the 1920s in New Orleans. It was followed by several other "lake" prefixed suburbs over the following decades. My generation entered the new area in the 1920s and 1930s, brought there by our enterprising parents. Our parents were the pioneers who bought and built their homes and raised their families in this ideal neighborhood. They could catch a cool breeze from the lake and enjoy green space between homes that the city could not offer. They watched their children grow in a safe and friendly environment. These children are who will tell you their stories in the following pages. Stories about growing up in Lakeview in the 20s, 30s, and 40s.

Many of the places and fun spots referred to in these stories no longer exist. Some of these places include the New Basin Canal, the Spanish Fort amusement park, Pontchartrain Beach, and, of course, the streetcars running along the New Basin Canal. Short descriptions of these places are included in the personal stories to give readers an idea of the changes that have occurred since Lakeview was developed. I have endeavored to describe, to the best of my memory with the help of many sources, the never-to-be-forgotten places that our generation enjoyed.

In 2005, I evacuated my Lakeview home for Hurricane Katrina. When I returned, many neighboring homes were destroyed. My home had to have its first story rebuilt. After meeting so many others with similar losses, I decided to write this collection of stories, not about the hurricane, but about the beginning of this unique neighborhood. My friends and I cried about what it meant to us who grew up here and to watch our fathers build homes when there were only a few streets in Lakeview. We enjoyed recounting stories about living among the weeds and trees and our new homes in the land made from a cypress swamp. I am not a research expert. I simply have gathered as many memories and pictures from all who wished to help. I extend my sincere thanks to each and everyone.

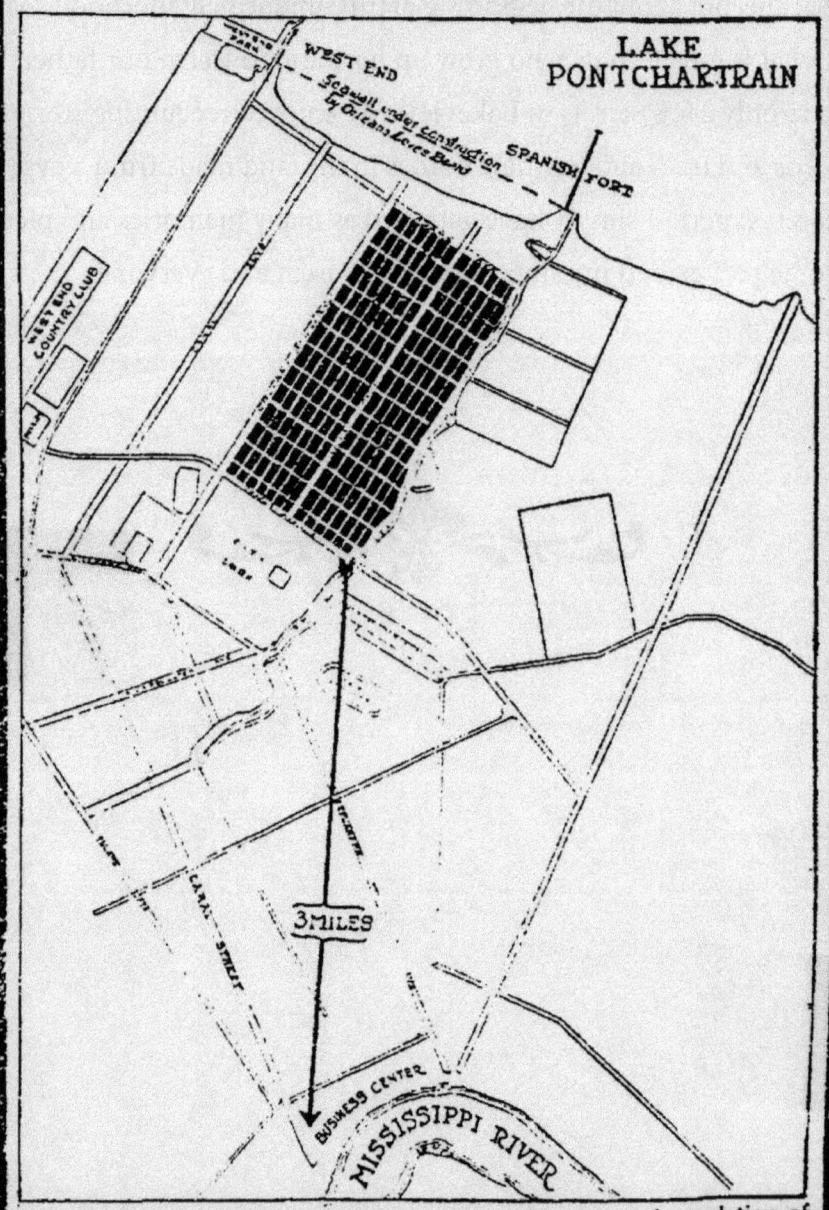

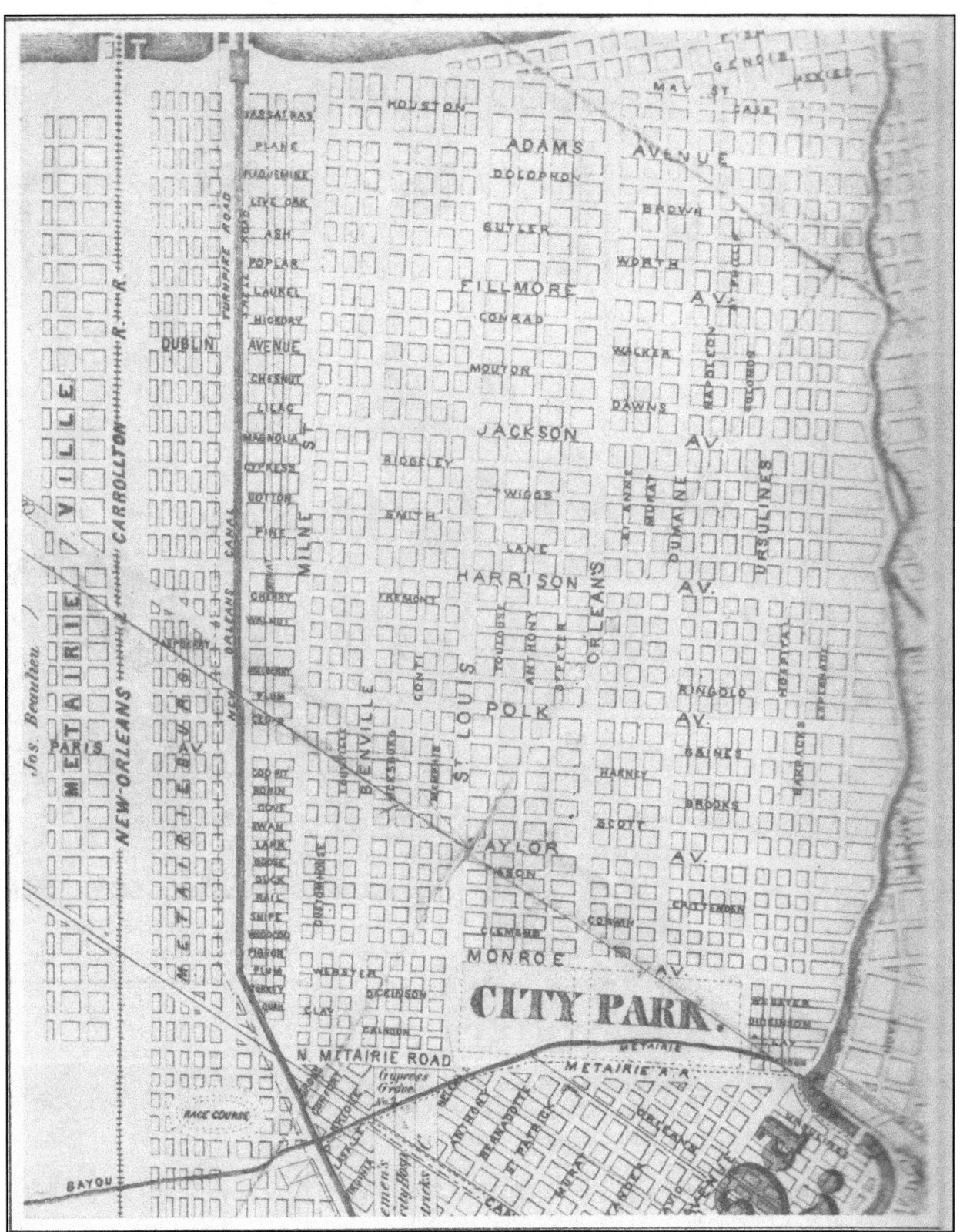

▲ Orleans Canal Pumping Station near Florida Avenue. Courtesy: Muriel B. MacHauer family.

▲ The first house erected in Lakeview in 1905, 6391 Julia Street, now West End Blvd. The house served as an office and tool storage for workers clearing the swamp. Photo in the Public Domain. Courtesy: Tulane University

▶ One of the first residences in Lakeview, 6745 West End Blvd. The house was build by W.A. Porteous in 1909. Photo in the Public Domain. Courtesy: Tulane University

PART II
Childhood Memories

MICHAEL J. ARTALL

Written by Antoinette Artall Costa, daughter of Michael J. Artall

I am writing about a man who had the foresight that Lakeview was an upcoming place to live and he decided to build his business on Harrison Avenue. At that time, Lakeview was mostly woods. Harrison Avenue was a canal with two streets on either side of it. The whole area was sparsely populated. This man was Michael J. Artall, my father. He was a pharmacist, graduated from Loyola University, and married my mother, Ange Roppola. They raised two daughters, my sister Lucille and me, Antoinette.

As early as the 1940s, my father and his cousin, John Napoli, pooled their money and bought an old house on Harrison Ave. They renovated it to become Harrison Drug Center. After a few years, they decided to build a larger store next to the old one and rented the older building to Humphrey's Bakery. The new drug store had a soda fountain, a delivery service, and employed several people. It kept the name, Harrison Drug Center, at 735 Harrison Avenue.

My parents later built on Canal Boulevard when the area of Lakeshore was developed.

When I graduated from Dominican College and was married in 1950, we built our home on Argonne Boulevard in Lakeview. It is there that I have lived with my husband, Victor Costa, for 62 years. We raised our three daughters, Karen, Judy, and Michelle. All of our daughters attended St. Dominic School, Mt Carmel Academy, and they made many friends in the neighborhood.

My husband and I have only fond memories of our happy life here. After the tremendous damage inflicted by Hurricane Katrina, we returned to rebuild and we enjoy the rest of our lives in this beautiful part of New Orleans, Lakeview.

Frances "Honey" Virgadamo Blondo

My parents, Antonio and Frances Virgadamo, were married in New Orleans. My father was from Sicily and my mother was a New Orleans girl. They moved into the newly opened subdivision called "Lakeview" somewhere before 1921. I am told that they lived on Orleans Avenue in 1921 when I, their first child, Frances, was born. There was no electricity in the house; therefore, oil lamps were used. I am not sure about the other utilities; although, I do remember we had a cistern to catch rainwater for drinking. In fact, everyone had cisterns, which were wooden tanks built high off of the ground and a screen covered the top.

The few houses and people who lived near us were all friendly, either relatives or close neighbors, and they were very helpful to each other. There were many, many vacant lots, and because my dad was a farmer, he simply cultivated all the area near and around to grow vegetables. Nearly everyone raised a few chickens and some people even had one or two goats for their own consumption. My dad even built a large brick outdoor oven where he could bake Italian bread. Others came to use his oven because he could bake as many as ten to twelve loaves at a time. We all helped my parents with the chores and my dad brought his vegetables by truck to the French Market to sell his produce along with many other people from surrounding towns.

The French Market was a really popular place, especially on Saturday when the inner city folks came with their baskets to buy fresh vegetables, fruit, meat, and seafood. There were stalls where the butchers cut the meat right in front of the customers. There were skinned rabbits hanging on hooks. The fish stalls were filled with tubs of shrimp and every kind of fish waiting to be cleaned to your instructions. There were bananas, which came right off of the boat parked nearby on the river straight from South America. So many people made a good living at the French Market.

Eventually, my father built his own house on Memphis Street. There were six children in our family. However, one sister died at six months of age from the terrible flu epidemic that hit New Orleans. Unfortunately, the house on Memphis Street burned and we had to leave Lakeview while my father rebuilt. This caused me to leave my first school, St. Dominic, and attend William France. When we returned to Lakeview, I attended Lakeview Public School until the 7th grade. The old building is still there on Milne Street as it sits abandoned now in 2010. I can remember only one girlfriend while in Lakeview School. Her name was Rita Talen and she was oh so pretty!

At that time, there were little corner stores just like the ones in inner New Orleans. My Aunt, Lena Virgadamo had the only corner grocery store on the east side of Canal Boulevard. My aunt worked very hard selling all the household and food supplies that we couldn't grow. Her store was on the corner of Harrison Avenue and Memphis. Similar to other stores, she raised her family upstairs and ran her business downstairs.

My childhood memories are happy ones living near most of my relatives who helped each other during the depression years. As children, we did not realize the hard times people faced. We were all treated with love and togetherness and had so many happy times enjoying our simple entertainments. My dad drove us all out to the small sandy beach out by the West End lighthouse. Here we jumped in and out of the water and played in the sand. I never did go out far enough to learn to swim. Other times we went to the big amusement park by Spanish Fort to picnic by the beach. Also, at night there were stage shows and air attractions to watch all for free. Once a year, there was a bathing beauty contest to pick a beauty to be crowned Miss New Orleans. That really drew the crowd.

After leaving 7th grade, girls from Lakeview either went to the nearest high school, which was John McDonough on Esplanade Avenue, or one of the Catholic schools like Dominican or Ursuline Academy or the only one in Lakeview, which was Mt. Carmel Academy. I went to work to help out the family.

Then by 1941, there came WWII, which changed everyone's lives. Girls my age were working and waiting for our sweethearts to return. As the story goes, I met and married a New Orleans boy returning from the service by the name of Joe Blondo. We lived on Cleveland and Johnson at first, but eventually returned to Lakeview, which was growing and building as fast as possible. We raised our family in the best part of New Orleans where there was space, and conveniences, and most of all memories of the happy times I had growing up here.

▲ Little girl's tea set. Courtesy: Muriel B. MacHauer family.

Merlin Bonie

I was not quite a New Years Baby. I waited and arrived on Jan 3, 1938 at the family home at 6901 General Haig Street. In those days, midwives were very busy delivering babies. My parents, like so many, believed that hospitals were full of germs and their babies should be delivered in their clean homes.

I grew up in Lakeview until I was 5 years old. It was then that my family moved to the uptown area of New Orleans. I still have a few interesting memories of living and playing in the old house surrounded by weeds and trees. My sister, Muriel, went to McMain High School and my sister, Virgilyn, went to Lakeview Elementary School. I stayed home and played with my pets until I was old enough to register at Allen Elementary School.

I remember one day that my brother, Walter, took Virgilyn and I for a walk in the woods. He had built a teepee made from bamboo. He told me to go in and sit down on a bench inside. Then he told me to come out and told Virgilyn to go in and sit down. When she was settled, he pulled a string that was tied to the top and the whole thing collapsed on top of her. I guess it was a lesson on how big brothers could tease little sisters.

Both of my sisters treated me like another little baby doll. Muriel took me on walks in my stroller and Virgilyn loved to paint my face with lipstick and rouge. But there was no, no, no dressing me like a baby girl. I would never allow it.

Like all kids in Lakeview, we often went picking blackberries knowing full well that snakes lived under the bushes. On one occasion, Virgilyn pulled me in my wagon. I was big enough for my feet to hang to the ground. Soon a snake decided to crawl over one of my feet. I froze and my sister froze too. Soon the snake crawled on past. My sister and I ran home as fast as we could, trembling all over.

We moved to Palmer Avenue in uptown New Orleans near Allen Elementary School. Virgilyn was told to hold my hand and never let it go as we walked to and from school. My whole life changed. No more wide-open spaces between houses, no more weeds. I had to get used to traffic and look both ways before crossing a street. Also, there were no more animals and pets. I missed country life. I had to get used to living in the city, but I had neighbors and many friends near home.

I grew up and attended Fortier High School. I studied Architecture at Tulane University. Now, I am busy in my profession and live in Lake Vista, which is very near to the home I was born in. I still look back to my days in that carefree -- almost a country town -- called "Lakeview."

▲ Merlin Bonie on hobby horse toy, 1940
Courtesy: Bonie Family

WALTER C. BONIE

My parents built their house in Lakeview in approximately 1923 or 1924. It was on the corner of General Haig and Mouton Streets, 6901 General Haig to be exact. General Haig was a street made of oyster shells and Mouton was not yet cut through. It was overgrown with trees and brush. Only when the WPA (Works Progress Administration) came along bringing gangs of men with tools to chop trees and cut weeds did we know there was to be a street built. They worked slowly and carefully smoothing the dirt and digging gutters on each side to make the area look like a street, but the mud was so soft that we could not even ride a bike on it.

I was the second of four children born in that house in Lakeview. My older sister was Muriel, then a sister named Virgilyn and then a brother named Merlin. I had a happy childhood feeling that I lived half in the country and half in the city. The whole area did not look like the modern suburb of today.

My daddy worked downtown and took the Robert E. Lee Bus and then the West End streetcar every day to work. On weekends, or days off, he played with us or took us in his open car to the beach or City Park or West End Park to watch the big fountain with colored lights or to eat crabs at the many seafood stands surrounding the park. He also liked to play jokes on us, which I will never forget. One evening he came home from work in an auto. We were somewhere indoors and did not notice. He walked into the house and announced that there was a pony in the backyard. We all jumped into the air, including my mother, and ran out to the garage. There was a new car, a Pontiac! What a letdown. Only my mother was thrilled. We expected to have a real live pony ride, never thinking about the care and upkeep. Of course, we were happy about the new car and loved him for the surprise.

My daddy's brother, Alfred, lived with us and, like all other neighbors, kept a vegetable garden on land next to the house. We also had a fenced yard for chickens and a spare one for ducks. During the Great Depression, people did everything they could to keep food on the table. We even had a pair of goats. The story behind that is that I was not a very strong kid. I always came down with a cold and even had pneumonia once or twice, so another uncle who was a medical doctor, Dr. Tedesco, recommended that I drink goat milk to make me strong. He even supplied the pair of goats that he brought from one of his other relatives. My Uncle Alfred had one more job. He tried to teach me to milk the nanny, but I could not. The milk was good, especially when my mother served it cold from the ice box.

There is another interesting story about the goat. My friends Robert and Lloyd Pope, our neighbors, tried to hitch the billy up to my wagon. I dressed up in a robe with a paper crown and played king in the parade. They pulled old billy with a rope and a carrot half way down the street when he decided he liked something better across the gutter. So there I went, costume, crown and all into the dirty gutter, the end of parade.

At that time, General Haig Street was covered with shells. In fact, it was the only street opened between Canal Boulevard and Orleans Street. Auto traffic made it smooth down the middle and kids rode bikes in the street. There were no sidewalks. I was not old enough to have my own two wheeled bike. Therefore, one day I took my sister's bike and tried to ride up the street. Needless to say, I came home with a big cut on my knee from falling on the oyster shells. My mother did the first-aid and we thought that in time it would heal. It took forever because infection set in and the doctor, my uncle, made me keep it immobile and my mother had to put some yellow poultice, probably sulphur, on it. That was one summer I spent on the back porch of the house waiting for my knee to heal. At that time, penicillin was unknown. My mother was extremely worried that I may have my lower leg cut off.

When I was old enough, I was so happy to start kindergarten in Lakeview School. I loved my teacher Miss Hezeau. I made many friends there. Some became lifelong friends. The Sadlier boys lived across the street from the school. They were Claus, Sterling, Ronald, and Jerry, who was my age. There was one sister, Alma, who is now known as Sister Anjelle, a Carmelite nun. The Sadlier boys became lifelong friends. We rode our bikes everywhere. We flew kites and made model planes together and later went to Warren Easton High School where I joined the band playing the French horn.

My parents enjoyed taking us to catch crabs in the lake. We went to the Chef Menteur bridge or to Fort Pike where we dropped nets off the small foot bridges leading into the fort. Another place my parents liked to take us was to the Spanish Fort Amusement Park where we could ride some rides, or swim in Lake Pontchartrain, enjoy the sand beach, and even watch the annual Miss New Orleans Bathing Beauty Contest. On one particular night, the winner was Miss Dorothy Lamour, who went on to become a popular movie star.

Lakeview, to me, meant a happy childhood. I enjoyed the West End streetcar and we'd ride downtown to buy clothes, the Sundays in City Park to hear the police band and watch the dancing schools give their performances on the stage by the building known as the "casino." There were the children's train rides and the paddle boats that we could rent to explore the lagoons.

I feel lucky to have grown up in such a nice neighborhood. Lakeview memories are all good. There were few houses, but we knew all of our neighbors. There was a great depression in our country. Our parents were all struggling, but we, as kids, lived without fear. Neighbors shared and cared about one another. Then when my parents moved uptown, I attended Tulane University and joined the Air Force during the Korean Conflict. Many changes took place all over the country. Lakeview grew with houses and businesses and people came to continue to enjoy this "almost suburb".

▲ "The Bonie Children" On the front lawn at 6901 Gen. Haig St. The four children of Walter Bonie, Virgilyn, Walter, Muriel and youngest Merlin. Courtesy: Bonie Family

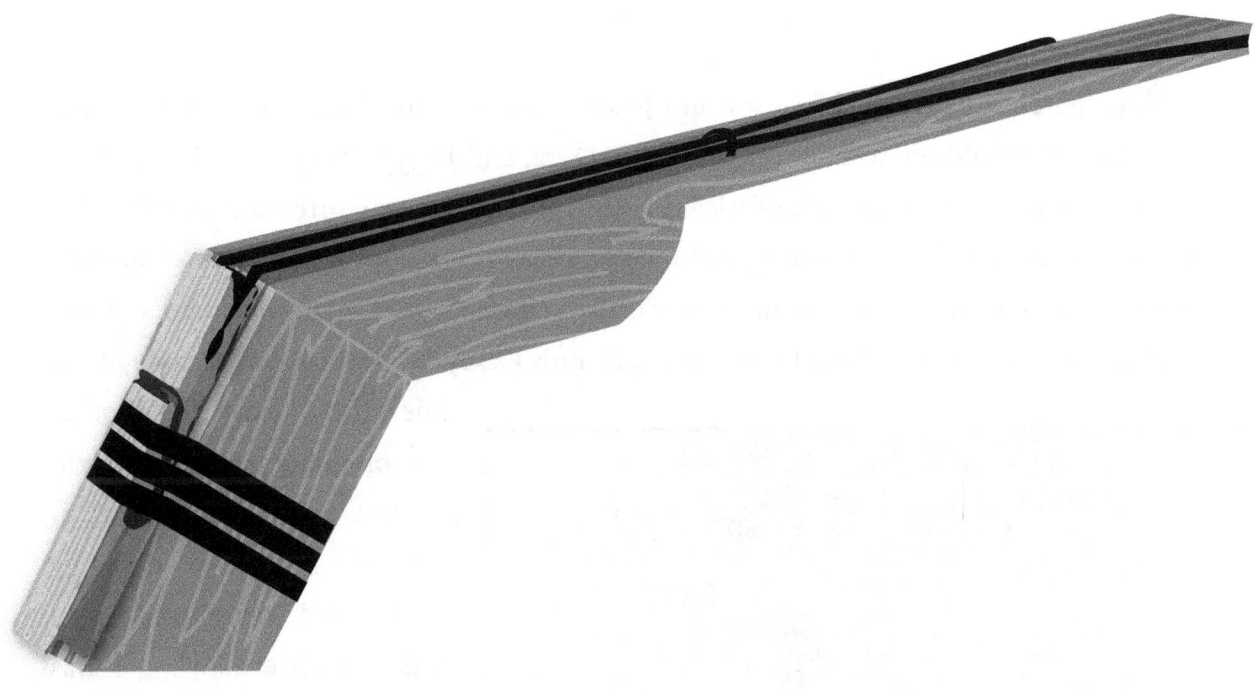

▲ "Rubberband Gun" A typical homemade toy called a rubberband gun. Children would use discarded inner tubes from atuos and cut them into large size rubberbands for amunition. Original sketch by Merlin Bonie, illustrated by Rachel Rivera. Courtesy: Bonie Family

THOMAS CASEY

Written by Thomas Casey

My parents, Dora Stubbs Casey and Joseph A. Casey, in 1931, moved to Lakeview with their five children, Joseph, Robert, John, Dora, and Peggy. They moved from their home in the Mid-City area of New Orleans at the corner of North Cortez and Iberville. My oldest brother, Joseph Stubbs Casey, was then 18 years of age. Our new home in Lakeview at 6000 Canal Boulevard was at the corner of Polk Avenue and Canal Boulevard and was a large residence and was built by my uncle, Dennis Casey, who was a contractor. At the time of that move, my mother was pregnant with her sixth and last child, me, Thomas. I was born on a great day, July 4, 1931 and was known as an "independence baby". I was told, by my older brothers and sisters, that the whole country celebrated my birthday.

◀ Casey Family Photo. Joseph A. Casey and wife, Dora Casey in middle surrounded by their six children. Back row: Roy, Joseph S., and John. Front row: Dora Casey Joubert, Thomas and Peggy Casey LeBlanc.
Courtesy: Casey Family

My mother gave birth to all six of her children at home. When I was ready for delivery, my mother called her doctor to assist. Dr. Richard was an old-time physician and he did not own an automobile. He had to take a streetcar from Mid-City to the cemetery area and he transferred to a Canal Boulevard bus. Public transportation moved slowly and Dr. Richard did not arrive timely. Consequently, my father, a lawyer, assisted in my birth.

Lakeview was a great and ideal area in which to grow up. The new Lakeview had numerous vacant lots for young kids to play sandlot baseball and football and plenty blackberry bushes to satisfy instant hunger. The neighborhood kids always had a glass jar to collect the blackberries. I will always remember the dark and black looking sand, which adorned the vacant land. The empty land was available to shoot Daisy Air Rifles, a.k.a bee-bee guns, until the city council adopted an ordinance, which prohibited firing weapons of any kind including bee-bee guns.

As young teenagers, we enjoyed hikes along the drainage canals and bayous and made frequent visits on foot or on bikes to City Park and the City Park swimming pool, which on a weekend was always very crowded.

My best friend and neighbor, Robert Upmor, and I bought a skiff and crab nets and frequently dropped the nets into Lake Pontchartrain. Bobby attended LSU, received his commission in the Air Force ROTC, and flew large Air Force transport planes.

I'll never forget the New Orleans Public Service streetcar, which always rocked side to side along the New Basin Canal, which is now West End Boulevard and was built mainly by Irish, to which many lost their lives constructing the canal.

Bobby Uptmor and I also built on one of the many empty lots a small shack out of black tar paper and would sleep overnight in the flimsy structure. There was an abundance of land for all sorts of outdoor activities and adventures in our growing up and our maturing process. It was all a great neighborhood farm area in a big city.

In front of our home on Canal Boulevard was the Canal Boulevard drainage canal, which was an open canal, but was closed, filled in, and beautified, when I was very young. In the process, the city fathers saved some landfill by making the beautiful sunken gardens between Polk Avenue and what is now I-610, which was a nice touch to fill in a canal.

Before, the installation of air-conditioning, the only relief from the heat was the use of oscillating fans and large window fans to suck the hot still air out and cause a breeze within our home. It was still hot, but at least we had a breeze.

▲ Casey Family Photo. Front Row: Dora, Joseph A., Claire Casey Levy. Back Row: Dennis, Loretta, Ruth and Byron Casey. Courtesy: Casey Family

THE CONNICK FAMILY

One of the most interesting and joyful tasks of collecting stories from people who grew up in Lakeview was my contact with a few members of the Connick family. Since there were eight children, this has to be a family story. This was a very close and devoutly Catholic family who still remain living under the moral principles of a good Irish theology. Most information has been supplied by brothers, Harry Sr. and Paul, since it would be extremely difficult to trace each one for an individual experience.

The parents, both from Mobile, Alabama, were known as Mr. and Mrs. James Paul Connick and were of Irish heritage and were good Catholics. They produced eight beautiful children, six boys, and two girls. Their father worked for the U.S. Corps of Engineers and served with the corps in WWII. The family settled in Lakeview in 1938. Their names were Jimmy, Harry, Johnny, Mary, Paul, Jessie, Billy, and Michael. According to Paul, it was a delightful experience to move into a big two-story house at 5835 West End Boulevard. Many of their early years were spent in New Orleans on Plum Street where they attended Mater Dolorosa Church and School. Then they moved into this large house with a vacant lot next door and a big grassy playground across the West End Boulevard. It was the area leading up to the bank of the New Basin Canal and the West End streetcar tracks. How wonderful it was to have a neighborhood swimming hole and a ball field for all to enjoy. So many happy memories remain for every member of this family.

This is the story of this close-knit family according to Paul. The oldest boy, Jimmy, was born in Mobile in 1924. He was baptized James Paul Connick, Jr.. He was fourteen years old when the family moved to Lakeview. He shared the fun with all of the kids in the neighborhood and loved outdoor sports on the green across from the house and summertime swimming in the New Basin Canal where schooners filled with watermelons came by carrying their produce to markets downtown. Often they tried every trick to get the men on the boats to toss them a melon, which they floated to shore to share with all their friends. There was a heavy railroad bridge, which would take trains across the New Basin Canal. Many times when the boats were ready to travel, the attendant raised the bridge high into the air so that the boat could pass.

▲ The Connick family, Mother Jessie and her children. Left to right: Michael, Jessie, Mary Genervive, Billy, Jessie and John. Courtesy: Connick Family

When the bridge stayed up waiting for another boat far away, brave boys climbed to the top to take a high dive into the canal. Whether or not mom or dad ever knew about this is unknown. After all, who would tell? Being the oldest, Jimmy loved and cared for his younger brothers and sisters. He was a truly a "brainy" guy and could win any word or math puzzle against the best of the lot. At age seventeen, he joined the U.S. Cavalry, which soon became mechanized. He saw action during WWII in Sicily and North Africa and, when wounded, returned home the same day that the Italian Army surrendered to the Allies. Jimmy attended Loyola Law School and then he, his wife, and his five children, moved to Lafayette and lived there until his early death at age 52.

The second son born to the Connick's in Mobile was baptized Joseph Harry Fowler Connick in 1926. This son, Harry, dictated his own story, which I transcribed. His early days were spent growing up in Mobile. Then, after moving to New Orleans along with the other children, he attended Mater Dolorosa School until the move to Lakeview. By his time, he was twelve years old, and along with all the others, he swam in the New Basin Canal and played ball with all the neighborhood kids. He remembers that there were always boys in and out of his family home. His mother was very hospitable and happy to have the house full of friends. There was a large screened back porch across the upstairs of the house and any number could stay and play. In fact, most mothers stayed home in those days and kids felt welcome everywhere. He attended St. Aloysius High School for one year and then attended Warren Easton High School. The family moved to Atlanta, so Harry attended and graduated from Russel High where he excelled in basketball and baseball. He also loved to sing and enjoyed the stage shows in Atlanta.

With WWII taking the minds and desires of all young men, Harry had to get into the action. In 1944 he joined the Navy. He was in action in the Pacific at Iwo Jima and Okinawa. When the war ended, he went to Japan twice and returned home in 1946. He attended Loyola University and then left to work in North Africa in Casablanca. Here he met Anita, a U.S. citizen, and they were married in Tangier and soon returned to New Orleans. Both Harry and Anita returned to their studies; Harry at Loyola and Anita at U.N.O. He graduated from Loyola with a degree in Business Education in 1958. Then he attended Tulane University Law School and graduated in 1961 while still living in Lakeview. He practiced law and soon joined the political field to become our well-known district attorney from 1974 to 2003. Anita became a judge. He remains in our history as a wonderful district attorney.

Harry and Anita had two children, Susanna and Harry Jr., who grew up in Lakeview and became most successful. Harry Jr., who grew up with music in his blood, is now a

Hollywood celebrity, a piano artist like his mother, and a singer like his father. He also made movies and has his own band. Susanna is now a doctor of Psychology living and practicing in Roanoke, Virginia with her husband and daughter.

Now that Harry has retired and Anita passed away in 1981, he resides with his new wife, Londa, in…can you guess? Lakeview, the land that we love.

John, the third son of the Connick family, was also born in Mobile. He was baptized John William Connick in 1928. He was only a year old when the family moved to Lakeview in 1928. He shared with his brothers all the delights and fun in Lakeview. He was a dreamer and romanticized about things he wanted to do and about what he wanted to be.

Paul says, "When we moved to Atlanta, we had occasion to visit Grand Park and the Capital Cyclorama depicting the Civil War Battle of Atlanta. Johnny was really taken by it and never gave up his interest in the war. When in school, he was so excited by WWII that he insisted on joining the Navy. Mama Connick was not inclined to let this happen. She had a husband and two sons already in harm's way and she was not about to let another one go. Dad finally gave in, so Johnny finally joined the Navy and was stationed in Washington State when WWII ended." He tells little more of Johnny's story except that he died a few years ago of "stroke and assorted maladies".

The fourth child born to the Connick's was christened Mary Genevieve in 1930. She spent her early years on Plum Street until 1938 when the family moved to Lakeview and attended St. Dominic and Mt. Carmel. According to Paul, she finished her nurse's training at Providence Hospital in Mobile, Alabama. She was a quintessential sister and from early on she was the "take charge girl and is still today. She is the one everyone turns to for help, directions, and diagnoses of whatever is ailing us, including mental problems. Mary will be there whenever she is needed."

Paul came along as the fifth child born to the Connick's. He was christened Paul David Connick, Sr. in Mater Dolorosa Church in 1931. He first attended Lusher Elementary on Willow Street and then went to Mater Dolorosa Catholic School. When the family moved to Lakeview, he was seven years old and attended St. Dominic School. At that time, the classrooms were above the church. The stairway had a landing half way up and Mother Gabriel, the principal, had her desk on this landing. Who could ever forget Mother Gabriel and her green ruler? If any rules were broken, you felt that ruler on your palms and a note went home for the parents to continue the disciplinary action. Besides the classrooms above the church, there was a small building in the rear called "the gray hall" where some classes met and was used for several meetings. He has fond memories of this school and the Carmelite nuns who taught him.

When the family moved into the big house in Lakeview, Paul was sitting on the front steps watching the movers and this kid came along and introduced himself as Rickie Villarubia who lived down the block. They became best friends and remain friends to this day. As good Catholic men, they still attend a retreat each year at Manresa Retreat House.

The move into Lakeview was most wonderful for a young boy. Neighbors and kids were most friendly and there was always a ball game on the green area along West End Boulevard and the bank of the New Basin Canal. Then there was the swimming spot all summer in the busy canal.

◀ Members of the Connick family seated on the front steps of their home, located 5835 West End Blvd. (1951) Left to right: Uncle Billy (standing) Aunt Marie, Mrs. Connick and Lt. Colonel James Connick of the U.S. Corp of Engineers.
Courtesy: Connick Family

▲ The Connick Home
Courtesy: Connick Family

LOIS JUNOD DAHLMAN

My parents moved into Lakeview when I was five years old, which would be around 1928. My two younger brothers were born in Lakeview. They were Louis and Milton. Milton is still around, but my brother Louis died in 2008.

My dad opened a hardware store on Canal Boulevard right next to the railroad tracks, which crossed Canal Boulevard near Homedale Avenue. It was the only hardware store in Lakeview and everyone who lived out there patronized my dad's store. We did not live above the store. Most store-owners in those days had living quarters above the business. We lived at 5736 Catina Street, which was not many blocks away. Next to his store was a dance studio owned by Hilda Cabbie. Next door to that was Fashbender's Barber Shop. Behind that store and facing Homedale Avenue was a barroom called "Homedale Bar". Across the street and at the corner of Homedale Avenue and Canal Boulevard was Johnny Falcon's Gas Station.

Dad sold so many items in his store that I could not count. I especially remember the kerosene for family oil lamps. Everyone had to have one handy because heavy storms often cut off electric power in the area. He also sold tar so people could repair roofs. He sold the usual things like nails, carpentry items, and paint. When they were old enough, my two brothers always helped in the store.

We all attended Lakeview Public School. This was the only public school in the area and we made friends with so many other children. Of course, the New Basin Canal was our swimming hole all summer. My mother cautioned me to stay out of the sun because my skin was covered with red freckles and my hair was a brilliant shade of red. Today, that would be extremely beautiful, but back then it made me extremely self-conscious. I do remember barge traffic on the canal and the watermelon boats. They were so loaded down that often my brothers were among the many boys swimming alongside until the men threw them a watermelon.

Announcing the Opening of
Junod Hardware

5500 CANAL BLVD.   GALVEZ 8720

ON OR ABOUT JUNE 1st

We will carry a well Assorted Stock of Hardware, Paints, Oils and Household Goods.

Our Goods will be Priced to Save you Money, and we will Give Prompt Delivery Service.

Give us a trial and save time and money.

See JUNOD HARDWARE
For Your Hardware and Household Requirements

Garden Hose	Paints	Bottle Cappers	Electric Fans
Garden Tools	Oils	Bottle Caps	Fishing Tackle
Brooms	Lime	Crocks	Step Ladders
Mops	Sand	Enamel Ware	Ice Cream Freezers
Galvanized Buckets	Cement	Tin Ware	Shovels
Galvanized Tubs	Roof Paint	Glass Ware	Spades
Galvanized Garbage Cans	Roofing	Screen Wire	Hoes
		Chicken Wire	
Flower Pots	Glass	Fencing	Rakes

And Hundreds Of Other Items

Come in and See Us

PHONE ORDERS WILL BE GIVEN PROMPT ATTENTION

GAlvez 8720   5500 Canal Blvd.

The Great Depression was very hard on my dad. He lost the business but stayed on working for the new owner. We moved into many houses in Lakeview, at least ten times, I'm sure. Each time we moved in a house it eventually got sold and we had to move again. I was always happy that we stayed in Lakeview.

No matter where we went, I always had my Lakeview friends to play with. I remember Shirley Messersmith and Donald and John. I also remember the Shert family of kids and especially their daughter, Joyce. In those days, large families lived in half of a double house. When we lived on West End Boulevard, my close friends, Loraine, and sister, Yvonne Rittner, plus their parents and Nanny, Mrs. Babin, all lived in the other half of a double house.

Our sports and entertainment consisted of riding our bikes out to Lake Pontchartrain and the lighthouse or to West End Park just to enjoy the cool breeze off of the lake. We also played tennis in the street on West End Boulevard. There was not much traffic then. Few people in Lakeview had cars and depended on the West End Streetcar to get them to work or to high school in New Orleans. It was always crowded during the rush hour coming home.

I did okay at the Lakeview School, but, sorry to say, I cannot remember the names of most of the teachers. I can never forget Miss Betzer, our principal, and how she rang that hand bell to call us in from the yard and, of course, Miss Maloney who had us sing the times tables every day until they were ingrained in our skulls. When I finished 7th grade, I rode the streetcar to Sophie Wright High School with my friend, Audrey Schwartzenburg. After riding the West End streetcar, we made four more changes to get to the school, which was uptown. In fact, one could ride all over the city transferring from one car to the next for only seven cents.

After graduating from high school, I worked for Liberty Insurance Company and married a Navy man named Dahlman. We lived on City Park Avenue in a small apartment very close to Lakeview. The marriage did not last, so in 1950 I moved back to Lakeview to live with my mother and dad at 6153 West End Boulevard and next to my old friends. I then decided to get a college degree at LSU and at age thirty I graduated and became a teacher in Jefferson Parish at J.C. Ellis Public School. I taught there until I retired in 1979. After I retired, I went on to teach at St. Raphael Catholic School.

I have many happy memories of my childhood in Lakeview. I felt the greatest change after Pearl Harbor when I sat on my front porch watching truckload after truckload of army troops being carried to the Port of Embarkation on the Mississippi. They were carrying our boys overseas to fight in WWII. It was new to me to see so much traffic in Lakeview. After the war, there were great changes that occurred in this big open blackberry patch where we enjoyed the country living. This was my childhood "wonderland". This is my happy memory of Lakeview.

▸ A child's favorite game of jacks. "Jacks"
© 2007 Lenore Edman.
Rights: Attribution 2.0 Generic.
Courtesy: Flickr.com

ALBERT J. DERBES

The following story is of a man of vision and development of Lakeview. It has been gathered from public records and from his grandchildren. He was of French heritage and a true family man. His generation worked to build Lakeview in the 1920s and 1930s. He was an attorney, a CPA, and secretary-treasurer of the already existing New Orleans Land Company. Mr. George Dedinger was president.

Many years prior to Mr. Derbes' time in 1831, before the Civil War, trade with Europe was picking up and it was difficult for large sailing ships to navigate the Mississippi River. The only waterway into the city was Bayou St. John. A new canal was needed, so the New Basin Canal was constructed. After the construction of the New Basin Canal was completed, the area between these two waterways was nothing but a marsh and a cypress swamp. This is what we presently call Lakeview. In 1887 there was an imaginative lawyer name Charles Louque, who did extensive research into converting swamp into land through pumping and draining. He is also known as the "Father of Lakeview." It took ten years to formulate plans, and with the appointment of Mr. A.C. Wuerpel as president, The New Orleans Land Reclamation Company was formed. Later the name changed to the New Orleans Land Company. By the early 1900s, maps were drawn and surveys for streets were made. Lots were advertised measuring 25 feet front and 150 feet deep. They were sold in pairs, so 50 feet in front facing the street cost $400. A corner lot cost $600.

Mr. Derbes purchased for himself both corners at the end of Canal Boulevard where it meets Robert E. Lee Boulevard and the bank at Lake Pontchartrain. On the west side of Canal Boulevard, he built his beautiful spacious home, and on the east side of Canal Boulevard, he built the Rockery Inn, which contained a restaurant, a hardware store, and a gas station. The name Rockery refers to the ballast from ships bringing produce up the Mississippi River and leaving their stones. These rocks were great for many things in New Orleans.

Mr. Derbes' home and garden on the east side of Canal Boulevard covered the whole square block where he lived and raised six children. His first wife named Louise Marie Delia Chadet died leaving one daughter name Delia. His second wife name Hazel de

▲ This is the home of Albert J. Derbes' family at 7040 Canal Boulevard, on the corner of Robert. E. Lee Boulevard. The home was built approximately in 1909. Courtesy: Derbes Family

▲ Another view of the Derbes home and the land surrounding the home, 7040 Canal Boulevard. Courtesy: Derbes Family

Generes bore five children. Their names were Albert Jr.., Arthur, Vincent, Vera, and Hazel. The family lived and enjoyed the cool breeze right off the lake. Mr. Derbes, along with a brother, also owned a fine yacht, which they kept in the New Basin Canal.

Mr. Derbes built and sold many pieces of property according to the booklet published to attract other buyers. I received a copy of this from his grandchildren. There are many pictures of the first homes built and the statements of contractors and builders. By 1908, Mr. Derbes built for himself another large home at the corner of West End Boulevard and Florida Avenue. Mr. John J. Castell built his very large home on Florida Avenue. Mr. Harry Romanski built his at 6315 West End Boulevard. Still remaining as of today known as "the house with the blue roof" at 6339 West End Boulevard, this house was designed by H. Jordan McKenzie and was his own residence. It was finally purchased by Dr. Clesi. Since Hurricane Katrina, it is now a historic landmark.

▲ The Derbes Family. Mr. Albert J. Derbes Sr., Mrs. Hazel Derbes and their children. Courtesy: Derbes Family

▲ Mr. Albert J. Derbes Sr. C.P.A. and Sec. Treasurer of New Orleans Land and Development Corp. 1920. Courtesy: Derbes Family

▶ This picture shows the intricate iron decoration at the front entrance of the Derbes home. The home was located at 7040 Canal Boulevard. The initials "AD" are displayed at the top of the iron door for Albert Derbes. Courtesy: Derbes Family

When the Great Depression of 1929 hit this country, Mr. Derbes, like so many others, lost his wealth and it took twenty years to sell most of his property to survive. He moved his family, wife, and six children, to Gentilly where his grandchildren grew up and were educated. He was known to be a very loving and generous grandfather. Each child remembers that whenever a birthday came up, or Christmas time, he gave each one a new silver dollar. He enjoyed taking them for rides in his big car many times.

When Lake Vista was developed, he moved there near some of his children until his death in 1961 at the age of 84.

▲ The ROCKERY INN
Lakeview's famous Rockery Inn was built by Mr. Derbes. It was located at the end of Canal Boulevard on Robert E. Lee Boulevard, situated across from his beautiful home. The Rockery Inn was a very popular night spot. The establishment had a bar, restaurant and dance floor. Cars would park around the building and were served by "car hops." The car hops would bring sandwiches and drinks to the waiting cars and attach trays to their open windows. The Rockery Inn was later purchased by the Signorelli family and they operated the business for many years. Courtesy: Lupo Enterprises

Rosemary McCoy Baudier Favalora

At the time that the new suburb called Lakeview was being developed, my parents thought it was an ideal place to build a home. It was a convenient place near the New Basin Canal, and near Lake Pontchartrain, so that their boat could be kept near our house. My dad and his friend, Mr. J. Casper Dodt, shared a boat called the "DOMAC". It was moored in the old Bayou St. John. The move to the New Basin Canal did not last very long, however, because people found it handy to fish or drop crab nets off of the boat and then leave garbage on the boat. Therefore, the move back to Bayou St. John turned out to be a safer idea.

My parents, Henry Joseph McCoy and Rose Angel Peyroux, lived in the half double house on Annunciation Street where I was born in 1924 and then they moved into Lakeview. They rented a half double while waiting for our house to be built at 6325 Catina Street. My sister, Beverly, was born one year later in 1925. The interesting story about our house was that our builder, Mr. Courget, finished building the house only to find that it was built on the wrong lot. Mr. Courget quickly bought the lot where our house was built. Thankfully, there were lots for sale everywhere.

Some of our first neighbors were the Messersmiths, who lived across the street between Ringold Street and Polk Avenue. Then there was my mother's brother, Joseph Armond Peyroux and his family, who lived on Milne Street just about a block away on the corner of Germain Street. Our builder, Mr. Courget, was his wife's cousin.

Even though I was very young, I have a clear memory of the 1927 Lakeview flood. I remember my father in his canoe paddling to rescue the neighbors and bringing them to the corner grocery store.

In the '20s, Lakeview had a few streets cut through, which were covered with oyster shells or gravel and there was a ditch on each side for drainage. The few sidewalks were built of wood by homeowners and were called "bankets" (a mispronunciation of the French word "banquette"). Two streets in my neighborhood had open canals down the center. They were Milne Street and Harrison Avenue. Where side streets intersected there were large wooden footbridges across them. There were only larger wooden bridges for cars at Harrison Avenue and Polk Avenue.

St. Dominic Church was located on Harrison Avenue at the corner of Catina Street on one side and the Milne Canal on the other side. It was a large two-story brick building with four large classrooms upstairs and the church downstairs. My sister, Beverly, and I attended the school from Primer through 7th grade. The 6th and 7th-grade classes were held in a small wooden building behind the church called the "little grey hall". Behind the building, there was another wooden house where the Carmelite nuns lived.

I can still remember some of the classmates that I had. There were two rows of Primer and two rows of 1st graders in our classroom. Father Paretta was our beloved pastor and his assistant was Father Lopez Perez. Both priests were from Spain and they lived in a large basement house across the parking lot from the church.

There were always children to play with during the summer vacation and after school. I did not learn to swim in the New Basin Canal as so many of my friends did. After work, my dad sometimes drove us out to the small sandy beach by the West End Lighthouse where we played in the clean, clear water of Lake Pontchartrain. My sister and I learned to play tennis at an early age in City Park at the courts where my dad coached us on Saturday mornings. He was a member of the tennis club. Beverly and I also took piano lessons from Mrs. Thelma Montegut in our home. We also studied elocution from Miss Violet Long and from the time I was two and a half years old I studied ballet and acrobats also. So you see, we had a very busy life as children.

After I completed classes at St. Dominic School, I attended Mt. Carmel Academy, which is also situated in Lakeview. It was a large three-story brick building on Robert E. Lee Boulevard overlooking Lake Pontchartrain. It was the largest structure on Robert E. Lee Boulevard. And over the banks of the lake, there were fishing camps and boats parked and occupied by their owners plying their trade. Beverly and I studied at Mt. Carmel until we graduated and then we attended Dominican College, which was in the section of New Orleans called "Uptown". This meant riding streetcars and buses and a number of transfers to get across town to get our education.

After attending Dominican College for one-and-a-half years, WWII started and I left and worked for my dad, who was with Davidson Dental Labs. Eventually, my father opened his own business and named it "McCoy Dental Labs". It is still in existence and is being operated by a grandson in its 70th year.

▲ St. Dominic's School Grades 2 and 3, 1932. Shown with Mother Superior Guidroz (1870-1946)
▼ The Mount Carmel Academy sophomore class. Years 1936 - 1937. Courtesy: Rosemary McCoy Baudier Favalora

While working with my father, I met Roger Baudier, Jr.., who also worked in a dental lab business. We corresponded all through WWII. He was with the Army Air Force and saw action in Italy. In May of 1946, we were married in St. Dominic Church. By that time, the church and school had been moved to its present site on Harrison Avenue between Vicksburg Street and Memphis Street. The school and gym were built first and Mass was held in the gym while the present church was being planned. So, we were married in the gym. We moved from Lakeview at that time and made our home on Pressburg Street in St. Raphael Parish and remained there for 24 years. We had six children. Our family consisted of four boys and two girls.

Roger and I had a very happy marriage raising our children in New Orleans and educating them in good Catholic schools. Then, in 1986, Roger died and I was left with my children and close family and friends. We all knew Fred Favaloro, who was a member of Cabrini Parish, and also our accountant for the family business. His wife had died several years before. We married in 1989. Our wedding was attended by 400 mutual friends and family. Archbishop Hannan and sixteen priests were also our friends that celebrated our nuptial Mass.

We continued working for the McCoy Dental Labs until age caught up with both of us and we now live happily in Jefferson Parish among family and friends.

My early life in Lakeview is one that I cherish and will never forget. It is part of me growing up in a section of New Orleans that was almost a country town and suburb since 1924. Today it is neither but is still a very beautiful populated part of New Orleans. I consider myself lucky to have had such a happy childhood with good parents in an unforgettable place.

▲ A picture of the Mount Carmel Academy May Queen Crowning. The May Queen is Miss Vera Cassagne (middle). On her left is little Rosemary McCoy, the attendant on the right is Loda May Eddy. Photo taken 1937. Courtesy: Rosemary McCoy Baudier Favalora

▲ The entire Mount Carmel Academy student body. Years 1936 - 1937.
▼ Mount Carmel Academy's French class. Years 1936 - 1937. Courtesy: Rosemary McCoy Baudier Favalora

ADELE YOST FOUCHEAU

When I was 7 years old, my parents moved to Lakeview with me and my sister, Jewel. We moved into our new home at 6208 Colbert Street. I remember the beautiful garden that my parents kept with 100 rose bushes. When they were all in bloom, I felt like I lived in a picture-perfect fairy tale. Daddy drove a Buick at that time so we did not depend on the West End Streetcar for all our outings. We only rode it to go shopping downtown or when we both attended McMain High School.

Before moving into Lakeview, we both attended grammar school at Mater Doloroso Catholic School in the Carrollton area of town. That was our parish church too. When we moved to Lakeview, we enrolled in St Dominic School, which was at the corner of Harrison Avenue and Milne. There were three classrooms above the church and more classrooms in the "grey hall" which was a wooden building behind the brick church. Sister Miriam, whom I loved, was my teacher for 3 years, the 5th, 6th, and 7th grades. My sister Jewel and I always walked to and from school. Since there were no sidewalks and very few houses, we walked through backyards taking whatever shortcuts that we found and then over a little wooden bridge crossing the Milne canal. I still remember that when we graduated from 7th grade there were 4 boys and 10 girls in my class. The boys were: Jules Cambre, P.J. Tooley, Nowell Baste, and Alfred Gilbert. The girls were: Althea Mae Clement, Alice Peyroux, Beverly McCoy, Marie Vadonvich, Anna Mae Treppenier, Vernon Haydel, Betty Prator, Chuckie Namious, Valerie Fitzgerald and me, Adele Yost. We were all a friendly group and so were our parents. It was like a second family.

We studied together and played games in the school yard, which included jump rope, hopscotch, and volleyball. The boys played their own games like marbles and ball games. Girls also played baseball and I joined the baseball team in 7th grade. We played against Sacred Heart School and next, there was a field next to the Water Works where we played Mater Dolorosa School. I was the pitcher. My dad bought me a softball to practice and play with, which I still have today. When we were ready to play, I saw two cousins of mine from Mater Dolorosa in the stands. They were Wilson Pollet and Shirley Pollet. They screamed and booed at me so much that I couldn't pitch a good game, so we lost.

My sister and I were not allowed to swim in the New Basin Canal like so many Lakeview kids. My dad usually drove us the West End Lighthouse where we enjoyed the small sandy beach on Lake Pontchartrain. Sometimes my parents drove us to the larger beach and amusement park at Spanish Fort where Bayou St. John entered Lake Pontchartrain. This was a long sandy beach with a big bathhouse and so many rides which each cost a nickel. There was one trip to this fun place that I will never forget. My father dropped us off there, giving each of us one quarter, one nickel, and two pennies. Then he left us saying we should use the nickel and two pennies to ride home. It turned out we spent all of our money and had to walk home. What a trip. First we walked down Robert E. Lee Boulevard, then down Canal Boulevard, then down Harrison Avenue and finally to our home on Colbert Street. We were scared to death because darkness came upon us. We were exhausted and my father was furious. We did not realize how scarce money was. One time we saved up enough to take the street car downtown on Saturday just to window shop. We put one penny into the Fortune Teller Scale and it said, "you will live to be 70". When my dad found out, I was lucky to live another day.

There were so many vacant lots around our house, so like our neighbors, we planted some kitchen vegetables. We loved to pick our own corn, carrots, string beans, and tomatoes. We also gathered wild blackberries for our mothers to bake pies. Of course, we always carried a long stick to ward off snakes. All of this came in handy as there was a terrible depression in the 1930s. As kids, we had no worries. We simply stayed happy among family, friends, and neighbors. This meant a lot to a kid growing up at that time. My daddy worked for the U.S. Post Office at that time and my mother at the V.A. Hospital.

After graduating from the 7th grade from Saint Dominic School, I attended McMain, an all girl public high school, located in uptown New Orleans. This meant that I rode the streetcars and buses coming and going. If I remember correctly, there were at least 4 transfers. We soon got used to it. For 7 cents, a person could ride all over town using transfers.

After graduating from McMain, I attended LSU in Baton Rouge at the age of 16. I truly wanted to study accounting or some profession. I loved to study and always did well in school, but my father insisted that this was for men. I should work, as other women, as an office clerk or nurse, which was women's work. I left LSU and attended Soule Business School. Times have really changed for women in my lifetime.

When WWII broke out, there was this boy in our neighborhood who worked at Hill's Grocery Store on Harrison Avenue. I did not see him at my school. We only talked. We did not go on a date. He joined the Army Air Corps. We began writing letters, and finally when he was discharged, we married. We moved into a half double that my parents had bought in Mid-City. For some reason, my parents had sold their house in Lakeview. We raised our little family of 3 daughters. Two were born in Mid-City and the third was born in St. Petersburg, Fla. My husband, Fred, worked for Pan Am Airlines. We transferred many times. Presently, after retirement, we moved in Metairie. My memories of Lakeview are all happy ones and I feel that having grown up in Lakeview was the best place I could imagine.

▲ "Spanish Fort, the Coney Island of New Orleans." A postcard depicting the Spanish Fort amusement park. Photo in the Public Domain. 1922. Courtesy: Wikipedia Commons

Patricia Howell Frost

My first memory of Lakeview is from 1935. My dad had just purchased a 1935 Dodge sedan and was taking us for a ride. We, meaning my parents, grandmother, sisters Gloria, Carol and I, were driving down Canal Boulevard, which was a one lane road that soon divided into two with a canal in between. There was a wooden bridge at Filmore. At that point, my grandmother exclaimed, "This is where your dad wants to take you to live?" The lot was overgrown with weeds and there was just one house across the street from our lots. We drove down what would become Louis XIV Street and turned back on Chapelle Street to the other side of Canal Boulevard to go home to Grandma's house in a more civilized part of New Orleans.

Our house was built of fine cypress wood, and in April 1941, we moved into it. This sturdy off-of-the-ground house had weathered many storms and is still there today standing straight and proud in spite of Katrina.

I remember going to my cousin Muriel's house on General Haig Street to play and we would cook Vienna sausage and scrambled eggs in her little playhouse in the backyard. I also had fun going to her birthday parties every year as well as having her come to mine.

The distance from our house to St. Dominic's Church was quite a walk, but we did a lot of walking then and the church was on the west side of Canal Boulevard. It was a two-story brick building with classrooms on the second floor of the school. It was located at the corner of Harrison Avenue and Catina Street. There again, Harrison Avenue had a canal right down the middle with weeds on either side of the canal. So many open lots in Lakeview were overgrown with weeds and blackberry bushes. I remember picking blackberries and chasing mosquito hawks for my biology class project.

Later St. Dominic moved the church and school to the east side of Canal Boulevard on the corner of Harrison Avenue and Vicksburg Street. While building was taking place, we went to Mass at the Lakeview Theater. Before the beautiful and big St. Dominic Church was built, which stands today, the school and building were built of red brick and the gymnasium was used as a temporary church. That is where my wedding took place

In the late '40s, Harrison Avenue began to grow. The canal was filled and business began to move in. I remember going to buy records at Studio A on the corner of Harrison Avenue and General Diaz Street. Harry Connick, Sr. complete with beard, was proprietor. I got to know the Connick family because my sister Gloria had become Mary Connick's best friend.

I attended Lakeview School for a short time, which is where I met John Frost, also a Lakeview boy whom I later married in 1947. My two sisters, Gloria, and Carol, attended Lakeview School from the beginning. It was called a grammar school, now known as an elementary school. It covered grades kindergarten through 7th grade.

To get to high school, I would walk to West End Boulevard to catch the streetcar. The waiting station was a small wooden covered building, which extended over the New Basin Canal. Then I would ride all the way to Broad Street where it crossed Canal Street, and I would transfer two more buses until I got to Nashville Avenue to attend McMain High School. My boyfriend, Johnny Frost, often rode with me on the same bus to get to S.J. Peters High School.

When Johnny returned from the service, we married and made our home in Lakeview where we raised our family until we moved into Metairie. My memories of Lakeview have all been happy ones.

Valerie Fitzgerald Gaffney

My parents moved to the beautiful suburb called Lakeview when I was about three years old. That would be 1927. It was sparsely populated, but it was away from the congested city of New Orleans and near the shores of Lake Pontchartrain where the cool breezes blew. Our house was located on Catina Street and on the corner of Harney Street. Actually, it was between the New Basin Canal and the Milne Canal. Lakeview had many canals, which were necessary to drain the water when we had heavy rains or flood. All houses at that time were built on piers to keep the floor off of the ground, or they were built high up with basements or places to park your car. Some basements had wooden floors where we could play games or have dances.

I had the experience of attending both St. Dominic Catholic School and later Lakeview Public School. The classrooms of St. Dominic School were built over St. Dominic Church, one of the first brick buildings in Lakeview. The church was located on Harrison Avenue, which had a canal down the middle, and Milne Street, which had a canal on one side. There were also classes in "the grey hall," which was a wooden building behind the church. It was sometimes used as an assembly and meeting hall. Behind the grey hall, and also facing Catina Street, was a house where the nuns lived. These women were our teachers. The priests lived in a large basement house along the Milne Canal. St. Dominic was a small school and we knew all of the kids. There was no cafeteria; therefore, at lunchtime, we either walked home for lunch or brought our lunch or went to Gordon's Grocery, which was across the Milne Canal facing St. Dominic Church and School. This canal was no wider than a large ditch with a wooden footbridge that made it easy for us to walk across. Mr. Gordon made sandwiches for us and I remember there was always a cat sleeping on the counter, which he had to chase off before making the sandwiches. There were no benches or tables outside the grocery, so we walked across Harrison Avenue Canal and sat on a big concrete mat next to the Hill's Grocery Store, which faced Gordon's Grocery. I think, this concrete box covered a cesspool or something. Few city facilities were built in this new suburb. We were lucky to have electricity and running water to all the houses.

My years at Lakeview School were just as interesting; although, there were many more

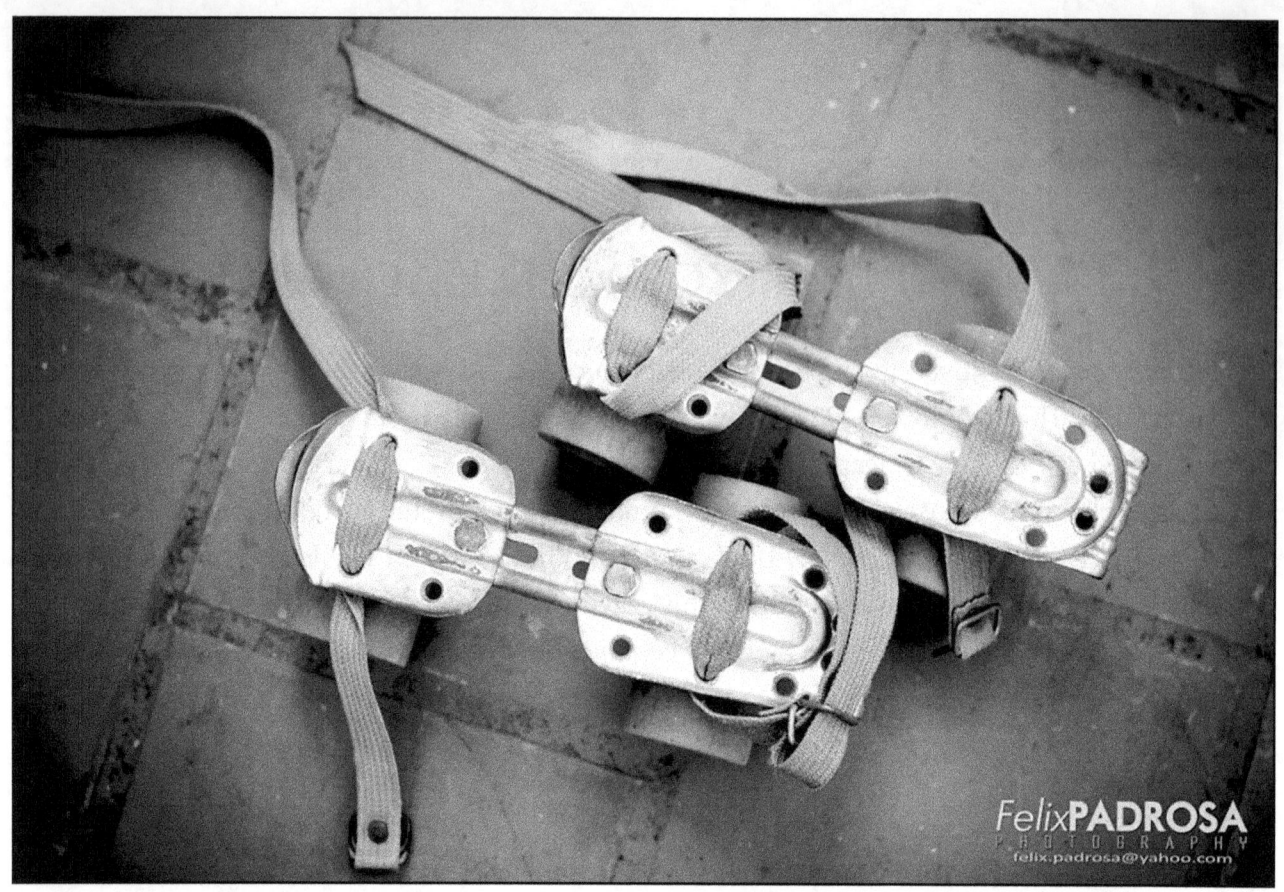

▲ A child's skates. "Old Rollers" © 2013 Felix Padrosa. Rights: Attribution 2.0 Generic. Courtesy: Flickr.com

students from kindergarten to 7th grade. The old school still stands today empty and abandoned. It was built of wood and painted grey. The front faced the Milne Canal and the rear street was Colbert Street. The school was shaped like a "U" and the center had a space for basketball or volleyball games or a stage where we had a May Festival every year. There was a cafeteria in the basement and an area where all classes met each morning to say the pledge, sing songs, and hear daily announcements by Miss Betzer, our principal.

The cafeteria served hot lunches for fifteen cents to kids who could afford to eat there and we sat on long benches by long tables. It was the time of the depression, so most kids carried lunch boxes and brought sandwiches from home or some stood in line for free sandwiches and milk provided by the Mother's Club, or some group of ladies, to serve the kids whose fathers were out of work. Being poor in those days was of no concern to us. We were all happy having fun together. Let me not forget Mr. Harry's Grocery across Colbert Street. For ten cents he served red beans and rice every day in a big room behind the store. There was another little grocery store on the corner of Colbert Street called Singletary's where Mrs. Singletary made French bread poor boys. For five cents, you got one meatball and lots of gravy, and for ten cents, two meatballs and gravy. Boys sat on the grass outside of her store with a sandwich and a big bottle of pop, which I thought would take the whole hour to finish.

Lunchtime was an hour long, so there was a lot of time to play outdoors until Miss Betzer rang the hand bell to get us back to class. The girls played jump rope, hopscotch, volleyball, or on rainy days, played jacks on the basement floor. The boys played mostly marbles on the hard clay ground. This meant drawing a circle with a finger and shooting their marbles to the middle, the rules of which I never understood. Most boys carried their marbles in a small cloth bag in their pocket, which would rattle when they walked into class. You could always tell the winner when their pockets were full.

Some empty lots between houses were overgrown with weeds and trees and blackberry bushes. Picking blackberries was a favorite summertime sport for most of us, especially when our mother could make blackberry pies. Besides carrying a basket, we always carried a large, heavy stick to chase away snakes who loved to hide under the bushes. Other empty lots were great to play softball and other outdoor games. The biggest spot for ball games was the green area between West End Boulevard and the West End streetcar tracks. This was mostly occupied by boys who had a game going on nearly every streetcar stop. As you ran up the walkway to get to the car stop, you walked across the tracks and waited in a little wooden shelter that was built half way over the water of the New Basin Canal. It was well built with benches and a good roof to keep you from the rain and a wooden rail to keep you from falling into the water. Of course, kids also used these stations to dive into the water for a swim. Most of us learned to swim in that canal. At first, my dad insisted on watching me and having a swimmer on each side in case I had trouble. My friend, Chucky Namius, and I spent many afternoons swimming here along with so many others. Some adults used to sit on benches in these little shelters and drop crab nets to catch big blue crabs. Knowing there were crabs in the water didn't bother us at all. Maybe it bothered the crabs. Besides being a recreation place for us, this station, and the West End streetcar, was our way to get downtown to the businesses on Canal Street. For us, it meant the only way to go with our mothers to get shoes and clothes.

Thinking of clothes, I'll never forget the Lakeview School's annual May Festival. Each class organized a little pageant or dance and the mother of the kids had to sew a simple costume like a colored skirt or shawl and boys wore big straw hats to look Mexican or from some other country. Most mothers, at that time, sewed and made their children's clothes. My class had a typical wedding and I was chosen to be the bride. This was a thrill for me, but not my mother. She could not sew. She was not too happy about having to buy me a pretty long white dress.

Later in my school days we moved to Memphis Street close to Florida Avenue. This was on the east side of Canal Boulevard and so I made friends with a whole new set of kids. My best friend became Shirley Uhalt. Her family owned a radio station called WDSU. They used Shirley's initials in the name. We spent many days together skating in City Park. After all, there were not many streets in Lakeview to use for skating. Most of the streets were covered with shells.

My high school days began and I enrolled at McMain Girls High School all the way uptown on South Claiborne Avenue. Most of the girls from Lakeview had to ride the West End streetcar and make four or five transfers to get to school. For me, it was too far to walk from Canal Boulevard to West End Boulevard to catch the streetcar, so a group of us met each morning and put up ten cents to ride a cab to school and took the streetcar to get home.

World War II came along and I finished my school days and married a boy named Gaffney and we lived on City Park Avenue until we moved to Catina Street in Lakeview. Here we raised our three children, so I guess I could say that Lakeview was my home most of my life and a happy one. It was in this beautiful suburb of New Orleans called Lakeview where the cool breezes blew in from Lake Pontchartrain.

◀ St. Dominic's School class of 1935. Courtesy: Rosemary McCoy Baudier Favalora

David Henry Machauer

As to be expected, there are many who grew up and spent their entire lives in Lakeview, but are no longer with us. Their stories are equally important and through memory and information gathered from close friends and relatives, I am including their stories to the best of my ability.

The first of these is the life of my dear husband, David MacHauer, who is remembered by many friends and family.

It was about 1920 or 1922 that his parents, Evered MacHauer and Georgia Drufner, married and moved into Lakeview at the corner of Florida and Catina Street. Georgia's parents, Aloysius and Rose Drufner left the Mid-City area and moved to Lakeview, their

▲ St. Dominic's School 2nd Grade Class. On left is shown First Pastor, Rev. P.L. Perretta, O.P. (Aprox. 1932). Courtesy: Rosemary McCoy Baudier Favalora

▲ St. Dominic's School 4th Grade Class. On left is shown First Pastor, Rev. P.L. Perretta, O.P. (Aprox. 1934). Courtesy: Rosemary McCopy Baudier Favalora

home was located on Polk Avenue and West End Boulevard. Around the same time, Georgia's brothers, Roger, and Donald moved their families to Lakeview on Polk Avenue also. Most of the Drufner family were living on Polk Avenue at that time.

David's parents had three children, Maryrose, David and Caroline Sue. David was born May 12, 1924. He and his sisters all attended St. Dominic School and Church and then located on the corner of Harrison Avenue and Milne. Both of these streets had canals running down the middle, which are now filled in with "neutral grounds". David became an altar boy serving Mass at the St. Dominic Church. He usually served with another boy named Jules Cambre. Both were the same age, but Jules was very tall for his age and David was very short for his. Together I thought they made an interesting pair, although, I did not know either boy at this time.

In his family, David was the lone boy, with two sisters, therefore, his parents gave him the task of watching over his younger sister, Sue, who always seemed to be getting lost or running into trouble. He had many friends in the neighborhood. To name a few, the

▲ Ribbon cutting ceremony at the South end of West End Boulevard. After the New Basin Canal was closed plans for an interstate system were formed. Shown in picture: Senator David MacHauer (center), left of David is Mrs. Mary Skelly Stumpf, President of the Lakeview Civic Improvement Association, on Stumpf's left, Mayor Chep Morrison of New Orleans. Courtesy: New Orleans Public Library

Connick brothers, Bob Roesler, Claude Spies, all of whom played ball on the large green that ran along West End Boulevard and the bank of the New Basin Canal. Of course, this was also the prime swimming spot all summer for all of the children living nearby. To their delight, there were the boats carrying watermelons from farms across the lake to the markets downtown. Boys had great fun teasing and begging the crew to toss them a melon so they could share and eat the delicious treat along the bank. A story that Bob Roesler loves to tell is that he and David often climbed the old black bridge when it was up to allow boats to pass. What fun it was to stand at the very top and do a high dive into the canal. Of course, they survived the dive and also the paddling that parents gave, if they found out.

David's parents' home had a large basement with a nice wooden floor. A local dancing teacher, Miss Oretlin, taught her students dance lessons regularly there. At other times, neighboring kids held little parties and dances there. All neighbors were friends and kids had a close relationship with each other. Most vacant lots were used for ball games or, if overgrown, there was blackberry picking.

When it was time for high school, David attended Fortier Boys Public School, which was located uptown, on Freret Street. Being the athletic type, or perhaps for lack of bus and streetcar fare, David rode his bicycle to and from school. He also delivered evening newspapers for the Times-Picayune-New Orleans States. After graduating from high school, he attended Loyola University and began to pursue a degree in law. I did not know David as a child since I lived far out on General Haig Street. We met on the West End streetcar while riding to college.

His education was interrupted by WWII and his anticipation to enter the fight. He joined the U.S. Air Force and soon shipped out to be stationed at the U.S. base in Lavenham, England. He served as a ball turret gunner on a B-17 and on December 24, 1944, during the Battle of the Bulge, his plane was shot down over Belgium. He was injured, but somehow survived and in 1945, returned to his home in Lakeview. He completed his education, getting a law degree. He and I were married and made our home in Lakeview, raising our four children. David entered politics and was elected State Senator representing the Lakeview area. Later he was elected New Orleans traffic judge when he and Judge Fonseca were the only two in New Orleans. His life was shortened by illness and in 1972, he died. He is buried in Greenwood Cemetery. I can truthfully say that he was happy growing up and chose to remain in the beautiful community and now rest here. With the passing of eighty to a hundred years and the progress of transportation using the railroad tracks and air to bring supplies and merchandise into New Orleans, the New Basin Canal was no longer necessary. The Louisiana Legislature passed a bill written by Senator David MacHauer to close the New Basin Canal in 1950, the same fun spot that he enjoyed as a child. It is now beautiful parkway with a Celtic Cross at the end of a memorial to the many Irish men who gave their lives to dig it. Many died from malaria, yellow fever, and cholera.

Muriel Bonie Machauer

After the swamp was drained in the early 1920s in the new subdivision called Lakeview, the New Orleans Land Company began to survey the area for streets and lots to be sold. My father purchased a $600 lot at the corner of General Haig Street and later what would be called Mouton Street. General Haig Street was an oyster-shell road a few blocks long. It ran from Filmore Avenue to Robert E. Lee Boulevard. My dad built his own home at 6901 General Haig Street of cypress boards with a private cesspool and a cypress cistern covered with a screen. By 1924, my father, Walter S. Bonie, and my mother, Evelyn Howell, brought me, a baby of six months, to live in this breezy lake area. There were few homes on General Haig Street, and our nearest neighbors were Mr. and Mrs. Nick Fury, whose home set behind ours facing the next street, Orleans Avenue, then better known as Turtleback Road. My dad and Mr. Fury cut the weeds behind the two houses and laid down a few planks for a walkway between the two backyards. Their two daughters, Josie, age fourteen, and Jennie, age twelve, were my only playmates. They treated me like a doll, dressing me up and rocking me. Our houses were built high off the ground on piers to protect from floods. We found this area under the house a good place to play and make mud pies, pretending to picnic using glass doll dishes.

I really loved my parents' large white house where I grew up. There was a large backyard and driveway with a large garage. The most useful part for all of us was the large screened back porch. In the summertime, it was our complete living area. We ate all of our meals there. My mother did all of her sewing there, and we played board games and cards far into the evenings with all of the bugs and mosquitos flying at the screen, wishing to get in. My parents kept a nice front lawn, and one day my mother brought home a small oak tree in a bucket. I remember watching her plant it in front of the house near the street. After Hurricane Katrina, while driving around Lakeview, I saw our enormous oak tree still standing and noticed that the present owner raised the original house and built a new lower floor.

By the time I was ready to attend Lakeview Public School, my mother had my baby brother, Walter. What a shock having a baby to steal attention from me! I also felt school was a place to meet so many kids my age! I was shy beyond reason and cried and hated it

▲ Mrs. Evelyn Bonie and first child Muriel Bonie on the front porch of their Lakeview home, 6901 Gen. Haig Street. 1928. Courtesy of Bonie and MacHauer families.

each day until my mother came to take me home. After a while, I grew and made friends and my mother later had my sister, Virgilyn, and my brother, Merlin. The girls who were my best friends then were Audrey Swartzenberg, Connie Hinkle, and Mary Meek. Happily, we are still close friends. Audrey lived nearby in Bucktown and Connie and Mary lived near Lakeview School. We visited on weekends, spending the day at our different houses, even though it was a long bike ride. My dad built a small one-room doll house in our backyard where I kept my dolls and playthings. When my friends came over, we played "ladies," wearing some of Mama's discards and high heels. My dad put in an electric light and an outlet to plug in a hot plate. Then we could cook pancakes and even fry an egg when my mother taught me how. Sometimes I spent the day at my friends' houses where we played with paper dolls or board games on the screened porches. I always loved the food cooked by different mothers. It was always a little different than my mother's.

Nearly everywhere in Lakeview there were vacant lots filled with trees and weeds. In summertime, we took a big stick and a pail to pick blackberries. The stick was needed to scare off snakes. All mothers made pies for us to enjoy.

Sometime in the 1930s, the seawall along Lake Pontchartrain was built. Many Mexicans, as well as men working with the WPA, built this seawall. It was very important to us. Sand and shells from the lake bottom were pumped in to build land from Robert E. Lee Boulevard to the seawall. Before that, the lake washed up to the levees by Robert E. Lee Boulevard and many fishing camps lined the shore. Where the seawall began at the West End lighthouse, there was a small beach. On warm summer afternoons, my mother drove me and my brother and sister to play in the sand and wade in the shallow water. The seawall was also enjoyed by men who came out after dark with their lanterns to throw shrimp nets for nighttime fishing. Older kids had watermelon parties there by the lake, enjoying the melon and then smearing each other with the leftover rind. They would then throw all the leftovers into the lake.

All of my friends went to Lakeview school until seventh grade. It was situated in a more populated area of Lakeview, and most of the kids either walked or rode bikes to school. The Lakeview neighborhood had another school, the private St. Dominic School, attached to St. Dominic Catholic Church. We always thought that kids who attended Catholic school were rich because their parents could afford tuition of three dollars a month. Remember, the '30s was the time of the Great Depression.

Surrounding Lakeview School was a real business world for me. At lunchtime, we could leave the school grounds and walk around the area. At one corner, there was Singletary's Grocery. This lady made the best meatball poor boy sandwiches in the world for only ten cents. Across Colbert Street, at the back of the school, there was Mr. Harry's grocery. His front display window had the largest variety of candy I had ever seen. Every day I bought a Tootsie Roll for a penny. At the rear of his store, there was a large kitchen with several long tables and benches. Every day his wife and daughters served red beans and rice to school kids for ten cents. There was always a waiting line outside. I ate there once. Mostly, I carried my lunch in a tin decorated lunch box with a thermos for milk. The school cafeteria was okay, but I did not go there often.

Behind the school, next to Mr. Harry's grocery, was Mr. Dulio's shoe repair shop. He had a thriving business because everyone had their shoes repaired there if they needed new heels or half soles and he always took pride in returning shoes to customers fully polished. Mr. Dulio and his wife were straight from Italy and spoke very little English. He had one son named Joe, who helped in the shop. Years later when Joe returned from military service, he took over the business and kept it going until he retired.

▲ Muriel MacHauer standing by the Oak tree in front of 6901 Gen. Haig, 2013. The tree was planted by Mrs. W.S. Bonie, her mother in 1929. Courtesy: Muriel B. MacHauer family.

Across the street from the shoe repair shop, and next to the school, was Mr. Evertte's pharmacy. Besides filling prescriptions, he sold a variety of things like perfume, powder, and comic books. In the same building, but on the left side, was a barbershop where most of the kids, including my brother, always went for a fifteen-cents haircut.

The street in front of the school was Milne Street, named after Alexander Milne, who owned most of the land around Lakeview. The Milne canal was always filled with green algae, so there was no catching minnows or anything in that canal. No kid played near it. We stayed on the school grounds, playing jump rope, dodge ball, or hopscotch. Boys carried bags of marbles and played at shooting them on circles that they made on the dirt ground. Many fights broke out over cheaters.

Girls carried a bag of jacks and a small ball, and we played in the school basement on the stage, which was often used for other activities. There was no such thing as playground equipment. It was a great day when they installed two basketball goals in the backyard.

There were two school buses servicing Lakeview School, probably independently operated. They were not painted yellow, the standard color of school buses. These had screens on the windows and wooden seats. One was called the Spanish Fort bus and the other was called the Bucktown bus. My mother would not allow me to ride the bus until I was a little older, maybe third or fourth grade, because kids were rough, and fights broke out over nothing, and she worried I might get hurt. Our principal, Miss Betzer, called the Bucktown bus the Bloody Nose bus, because she always had to have Band-Aids ready to give first aid after an early morning disagreement.

The Bucktown bus picked up kids who lived in the camps and fishing village on the 17th Street Canal, and a few came from the small neighborhood along Pontchartrain Boulevard. The Spanish Fort bus picked up kids from the Over the Rhine Restaurant, which was located on Bayou St. John across from the ruins of the old Spanish Fort. The kids along General Haig Street, Filmore Avenue, and all points in between, boarded the bus with the last stop being the corner of Harrison Avenue and Vicksburg Street. At this stop, the bus really loaded up with Italian children. The whole area on either side of the Harrison canal was known as Little Italy, only because so many Italian families lived there in small homes. They grew vegetables and raised chickens, ducks, and goats on all vacant lots near their homes. There were even outdoor ovens built like clay beehives where they baked delicious Italian bread. I made many friends with kids from this area. Although the United States was suffering through the Great Depression, Italian families knew how to survive.

When the school day began each morning, we lined up in the basement according to grade. We pledged the flag and listened to announcements from our principal, Miss Betzer. Sometimes there was a short poem or talk about a particular holiday. After this, we sang one or two songs from the good old "Twice 55" song book. Finally, one ring of the bell, and Miss Pecoraro, the music teacher, played a patriotic march on the piano while we marched very orderly and quietly upstairs to our classrooms. Miss Pecoraro taught music appreciation and had a helper named Ray McNamara, a young boy who could play the piano and who took her place many mornings.

Our teachers were very strict, though some were extremely nice and patient. The only behavior problems were from the boys. Some teachers singled out certain problem boys and had them sit next to the teacher's desk to keep an eye on them and give them a quick tap with a wooden ruler. Miss Remack had a particular tall, gawky student named Robert. He was so clumsy that he made it a point to fall into the room, knocking over a few desks, or pushing girls' books to the floor as he passed through the room. Miss Farsman, our History teacher, had a problem student named Eddy Williams. He was a really tough kid doing every trick in the book to make the teacher upset. She insisted on boys wearing neckties when they came into her classroom. If a boy showed up in her room without a tie, she furnished a black tie and made him put it on in front of the class and write the multiplication tables fifty times. At the end of class, she took her tie back. Eddy, of course, forgot his tie many days and once in a while, made a paper plane out of the times tables that he wrote and sailed it across the room.

Every year the school had a May festival and each class either did a group dance or sang a group song on the stage. Our mothers furnished the costumes, sometimes made of paper. The kids who had a special talent for singing or dancing were given a solo. My special friend, Audrey, who took dancing lessons, always did a great number of either tap or Spanish Dance. There was a boy named Louis Kiefer, who also took lessons, and they did a duet together. I remember a great little acrobat named Dottie Genelione, who always gave a great performance. The musically talented girls were the Ellison sisters, who played the xylophone, which was entertaining.

Many booths were arranged by the mother's club. They sold refreshments, cakes, muffins, handmade doll clothes, crochet, and small sewing items. Then there was the "white elephant" booth where parents sold many small items.

The New Orleans Recreation Department (NORD) sponsored a parade during Mardi Gras season from Lakeview beginning at City Park Avenue and traveling up Canal Street. It consisted of small floats decorated and pulled by boys from the many grammar schools participating. Two or three girls got to ride on the floats. The floats were about the size of a small pick-up truck and were pulled by seventh and eighth grade boys. One year Lakeview School had the honor of having one of their boys chosen as king. His name was Troy Svenson, and being quite handsome, was the heartthrob of the seventh grade girls. His costume was beautiful with a gold crown and a long train edged in fur. Also, a seventh grade girl, Doris Berthelot, was a beautiful queen on a separate float. I am not sure of the route of the parade down Canal Street, but we all went to line the street to see our Lakeview School king's float and separate queen's float. The following year at the May festival, the whole pageant, including queen and maids, paraded on the outdoor stage for all of the parents to see.

Going back to the neighborhood surrounding Lakeview School, at the corner of Colbert and Polk streets, there was a grocery owned by the Bongivanni family. The grocer was a butcher and very proud of his trade. Many times he was asked what made his ground meat so good. He would hold up his bent thumb saying, "Oops, there went another thumb." There was a two-story building that was also on the corner of Polk across from Milne canal that still stands today. At that time, it was called Price's Pharmacy with living quarters upstairs and business downstairs. Later it became a variety store run by Mrs. Drufner. She was called Aunt Marie and later became my aunt through marriage.

Many afternoons the children from Lakeview School who were Catholic walked along the Milne canal toward Harrison Avenue to St. Dominic Church to take catechism lessons from the Carmelite nuns who lived behind St. Dominic School. The classroom where we met was called the gray hall. These nuns taught at St. Dominic School and stayed extra time to teach us catechism. The only time I ever met the St. Dominic kids was when I joined the Girls Sodality or when we made our First Communion and our Confirmation. We had to practice lining up and walking in church with our fine white dresses and white veils all handmade by our mothers.

After catechism lessons, I usually walked home with a few other girls from the Filmore area. It consisted of a walk along the Harrison canal to Canal Boulevard, which was two separate lanes of black-top road with a canal down the middle. We walked down Canal Boulevard to the first cross street, which was Filmore, a gravel road. My friend, Dotsie Balaski, said goodbye at that corner. She walked down Canal Boulevard until she reached her parents' little business selling cold drinks, hot dogs, and candy. This was the only structure between Filmore and Robert E. Lee Boulevard. In the rear of the shop were the living quarters for her family. I say this to explain how few houses were on Canal Boulevard. I have fond memories of walking home on those evenings, especially when we passed a house and could smell supper cooking. All mothers stayed home at that time and had supper around that time of the evening. Most dads rode the street car home and brought the daily paper. We kids waited to read the latest comics.

By the end of seventh grade, we graduated from Lakeview School. We had a choice of a public high school for girls and another for boys. Most of the girls attended McMain High School or McDonogh 35, or one of the Catholic high schools. Although I did not attend Mount Carmel Academy, the only Catholic girls high school in Lakeview, it was a landmark to me. It was the only three-story building on Robert E. Lee Boulevard between West End Boulevard and Canal Boulevard. There were camps over the lake on the north side of the bank and vacant land on each side of Mount Carmel.

So many of the girls growing up in Lakeview went to Mount Carmel that I feel it is a part of our generation. Built in 1926, it was the dream of Mother Clare Cody to move the Carmelite nuns, a French order of nuns, to a new motherhouse in this new subdivision by the lake. It was a shock to leave the old building in the French Quarter. Many called it Mother Cody's Folly, but she was a determined lady. At first, they trained young ladies for teaching jobs, then it developed into a fine high school for girls and happily remains one of the best in New Orleans. The boys usually attended Warren Easton, Fortier High, or the Catholic all-boys Jesuit High School. There were no co-ed high schools in the 1940s. My best friends, Mary and Connie, attended McMain with me. My other friend, Audrey, attended Sophie B. Wright High School. These two schools were uptown schools, which meant learning to ride the street cars and buses and transferring at least five times each way. The street car was not new to me. When I was small, my mother took me downtown to buy shoes and other things. She always dressed up with a hat, gloves, high heels, and make-up.

The West End Boulevard car brings me back to one of my fondest memories of Lakeview. For seven cents, you could ride from the bridge where the New Basin Canal meets Lake Pontchartrain all the way to the beginning of Canal Street where it meets the Mississippi River. Traveling along the bank of the New Basin Canal, the cars would sway back and forth, giving a rocking feeling that you could fall right into the canal. Many people parked boats in the canal and lived in the large fine homes along West End Boulevard. Many barges traveled this canal, carrying produce such as watermelons and vegetables from the farms in Mandeville and Madisonville, which were small towns along the north shore of the lake. This canal ended in New Orleans' inner city near Howard Avenue, where there was the turning basin.

The street car traveling along the New Basin Canal stopped at a little wooden shelter where houses were built out over the water. There were benches where people rested while waiting for the cars.

On Saturday and Sunday evening, my dad drove us to the beach by Spanish Fort. There was a large beach and an amusement park built mostly over the water. We enjoyed rides like the bumper cars, the whip, and a roller coaster. There were many stands selling drinks, hot dogs, and popcorn. The large stage had free entertainment, like circus acts. Much later when I was a teen, the entire amusement park was moved to the end of Elysian Fields Avenue where there was a much larger beach and an old lighthouse. The lighthouse stood by the entrance of the new Pontchartrain Beach. At present, the whole area is now the campus of the University of New Orleans.

Another popular swimming spot and highlight of my childhood was City Park. The swimming pool was very well kept with lifeguards and diving boards. I enjoyed going there with my friends as I grew up. We rode the little train traveling a few miles under the oaks and the "flying horses," presently known as a carousel. There was a little wading pool, no more than one-foot deep, where little kids splashed in and out. On Sunday nights, my parents drove us to the free entertainment by the big bandstand in front of the casino. The refreshments sold at the casino were popcorn or an ice cream cone for a nickel. In those days, we did not have many nickels.

There was a boat rental behind the casino near the lagoon. My generation spent many hours enjoying City Park. It was a rare occasion to go to Audubon Park. It had much the same entertainment, but the biggest attraction at that park was the zoo. The zoo is still there, only larger.

West End Boulevard came to an end where the railroad track cut across the New Basin Canal. It has become a super highway, or expressway, which brings traffic from Interstate 10 into New Orleans. Before all of these changes and progress, there was a huge bridge, which was entirely built for rail traffic, taking trains across the canal into neighboring Jefferson Parish. This bridge stayed mostly upright, since there was more boat traffic passing under than rail traffic. Everyone in Lakeview called it the Black Bridge. Often when the bridge was up, boys would climb high to the top and use it as a high-dive into the canal. Two daredevils that I remember were Bob Roesler and David MacHauer. They would stand poised for a moment as the street car passed. Then making big swan dives, they plunged into the water, never thinking of the consequences.

After the street car passed the Black Bridge, it traveled along the fence of the Greenwood Cemetery until it reached City Park Avenue. At this point, there was a stop before turning on City Park Avenue to the beginning of Canal Street, which eventually brings the car straight to the Mississippi River. Back at the stop on City Park Avenue, there was a large ice cream parlor called the Double Dip. The old building is gone now, and the expressway is in its place. I'm sure every kid in Lakeview has memories of the wonderful ice cream cones sold there for ten cents.

The New Basin Canal no longer exists. By 1950, most water travel was replaced by railroads, trucks, and automobiles. The members of the Louisiana Legislature passed a bill to close the canal. Presently, there is a beautiful parkway in this area bounded on the east side by West End Boulevard and on the west side by Pontchartrain Boulevard. The bill was written by Senator David MacHauer, who happened to be one of the boys who grew up enjoying the New Basin Canal. Near the north end of the parkway is a monument that was carved in Ireland and donated by the Irish Cultural Society of New Orleans. It is a Celtic cross, honoring the many Irish immigrants who died of yellow fever and cholera while digging the canal. Surrounding the cross are four white stone blocks. These were found while filling the canal and had been used to support the sidewalls.

I feel lucky to have grown up in a place like Lakeview on the north edge of the city. It felt more like a country town than a suburb. Most families kept farm animals, such as chickens, ducks, and goats and planted vegetable gardens. Now one could call it a neighborhood. By the end of World War II in 1945, more streets were laid and more houses built. By the time Hurricane Katrina hit, hardly a vacant lot existed. All of Lakeview was developed. Veterans Highway was built and dedicated to the boys returning from the war. Now it is dedicated to all veterans. Down Veterans Highway and over the 17th Street Canal, is Jefferson Parish. The area between Pontchartrain Boulevard and the canal was a huge cypress swamp. Most of the houses in that area were built in the 1950s. It is now called West Lakeview.

I will always remember Lakeview as a special place in which to grow up. Picking blackberries in the summertime, climbing the bank of the Orleans canal to pick Iris lilies, watching various wagons with vegetables and drivers shouting their wares are my fondest

▲ A pencil sketch by Muriel MacHauer of the West End streetcar line along the New Basin Canal.

memories. Let us not forget the ice man who carried a block of ice into our house and placed it into our ice box while I and the other kids waited for the man to cut a small piece for us to lick.

Hopefully, others who submit stories will mention places and local spots that I may have omitted. To name a few: The drive-in theater at the corner of Robert E. Lee Boulevard and Canal Boulevard; the Rockery Inn and Lenfant's, where car hops delivered sandwiches and drinks right to the cars and where they hooked up trays and loudspeakers played music while we ate; Caruso's vegetable stand by the railroad tracks, which gradually grew into a small market. Sylvester's Grocery on the other side of the tracks was the nearest super store I can imagine.

Many old landmarks still remain, and in spite of the flood following Hurricane Katrina, many of us also remain to tell our stories.

With the passing of time, so many changes have taken place. I only hope that I have been able to share my memories of a neighborhood that was once so good and now even better.

▲ Child's toy wagon. ©iCollector.com. Courtesy: Jane Coogan

BETTY WITCHER MCMAHON

We lived a simple life in Lakeview where I grew up. We were surrounded by love. It gave all of us a good foundation. Memories are wonderful and remain a good part of my life.

My parents were both from Lakeview. They were Charles Swanson Witcher and Lily Sebastian Campbell and were married in 1923. Their first home was built at 5650 Woodlawn Street, where their four children were born. My three brothers are Charles, Robert, and Richard, and I am Betty.

In 1930 we moved to my father's mother's home at 5670 Hawthorne Street. There were 36 children in that block. We had good old-fashioned fun together, skating, playing jacks and so many games. The boys played ball and swam in the New Basin Canal. Another favorite swim spot was in Lake Pontchartrain next to the West End lighthouse. There was a small sandy beach and a safe spot for children to play. The lighthouse was at the entrance to the New Basin Canal to guide boats from the lake to the canal. After a nice swim, we went to Bart's Restaurant for refreshments, which was next to the lighthouse.

We lived so close to Lakeview School on Milne Street that we walked to school every day with our friends joining us. There were many children who lived across the New Basin Canal. Their father rowed a boat across the canal to get them to school.

One of my fondest memories was of Mrs. Singeltary's corner grocery, near school. She made and sold the most delicious sandwiches on French bread. I especially liked a banana sandwich and still enjoy them today. Another was meatball with lots of gravy. One meatball sandwich sold for five cents and two meatballs sold for ten cents.

President Franklin D. Roosevelt visited New Orleans once, and we were taken to Canal Boulevard near City Park Avenue and waved American flags when he passed by in his open car motorcade. Years later, another US president visited New Orleans. We went to the airport to see President John F. Kennedy when he visited. He shook hands with our little son, Robert.

Another event in my memory to cause excitement was when a piece of a star fell on Canal Boulevard. Everyone had to rush out to see it. It remains there today with a plaque to mark the place. It is now called a piece of meteorite.

Back in the 1940's, merchants drove trucks through the streets, selling fruit and vegetables. One driver, Mr. Trumbino, called out loud and clear, describing what he was selling. The ice man also came in his truck, delivering ice into everyone's ice box to keep food cool for a short time. He sold fifty pounds for ten cents. We all gathered around his truck waiting for him to hand out large chips to keep us cool.

In 1927, the Mississippi River levee broke and flooded New Orleans. Citizens went out in boats, and children in bathing suits to play in the water. Adults used skiffs to get to the groceries or to carry relatives to their homes.

It was a real treat to go to Pontchartrain Beach Amusement Park, where we swam and enjoyed the many rides and refreshments. This is where beauty and big band concerts were held.

Near the West End lighthouse was a place called Krupp's. The Krupp family sold sandwiches, cold drinks, snow balls, and slices of watermelon. We sat on benches with picnic tables facing the cool waters of Lake Pontchartrain. In front of Krupp's on the seawall, there was a high white lifeguard chair manned by P.J. Krupp or other fine young Lakeview men.

Another enjoyable summertime spot was across the New Basin Canal. It was West End Park. It was a small park with swings and picnic tables. In the center, there was a large fountain. An attendant came at nighttime and operated colored lights, giving us a dancing water show while people sat on benches enjoying the breeze.

On the dark side, there was the well-known 1929 Great Depression, where banks froze and kept any savings we had. Some people lost their homes and their jobs. Somehow our parents managed, and we survived on less, but as children most of us continued our happy days with our many playmates.

I met a Mid-City boy named Bob McMahon before World War II. Our country entered the war at the time we were all trying to get educated. Bob soon joined the US Army. He saw much action, first in Cuba, then Guam and finally Japan. He was wounded twice and miraculously survived heavy combat to save our country. After the war ended, we were married in 1947 by a friend of Bob's, Father Buddy Benedix. We settled in Lakeview in our family home at 5933 Catina Street.

While our boys were fighting, the girls continued getting an education. After Lakeview School, I attended Sophie B. Wright High School on Napoleon Avenue. From there, I attended and graduated from Joseph Maybin Business School. I was employed at the Federal Reserve Bank initially, then I joined the Jefferson Parish school system, teaching special education children for thirteen years.

Bob and I were blessed with four children. They included one son, Robert Jr., and three daughters, Mary Beth, Jane, and Barbara. We lived a happy family life in Lakeview on Catina Street until Hurricane Katrina destroyed our lovely home in 2005. All is changed now, but fortunately we survived. We still cherish our happy memories of our early days in Lakeview.

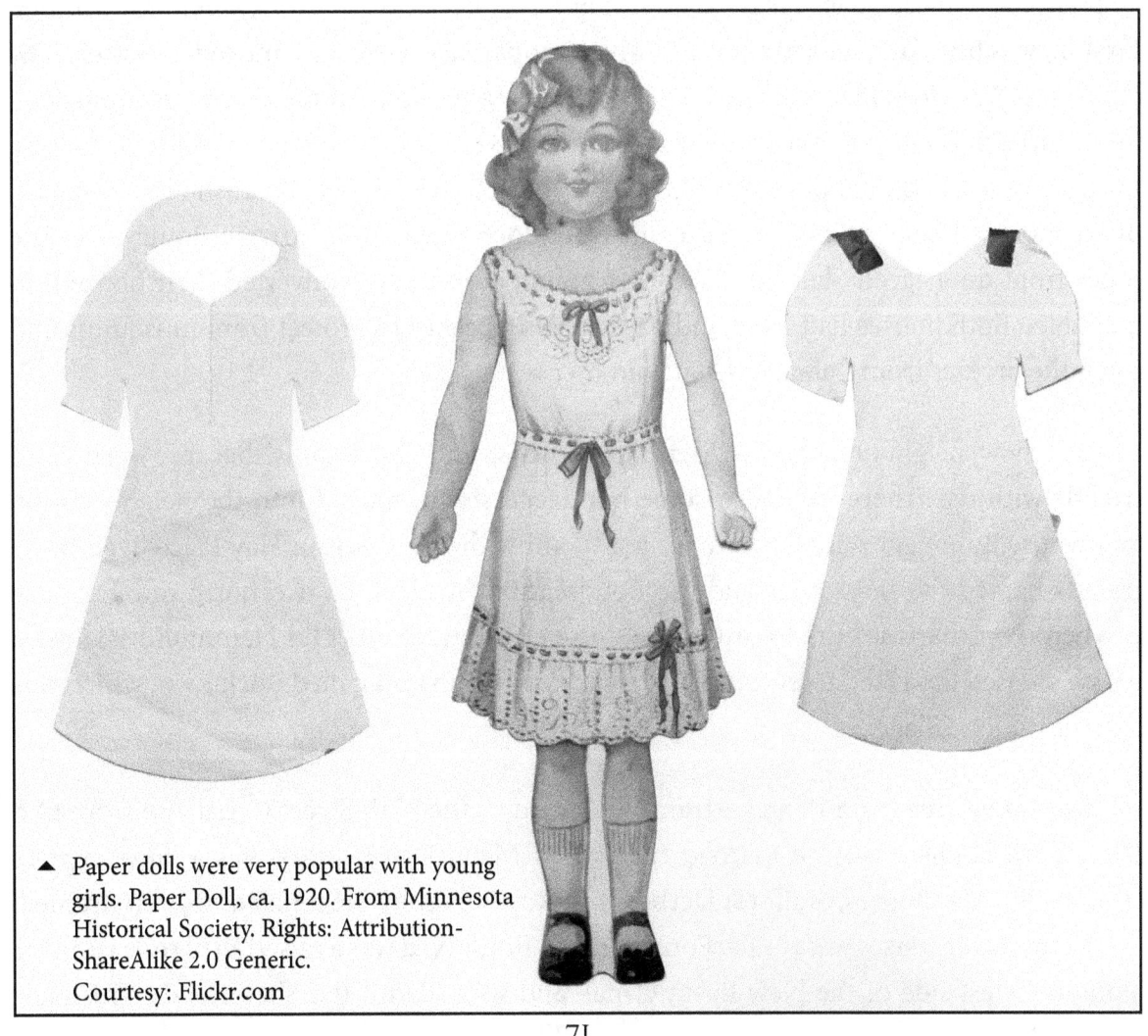

▲ Paper dolls were very popular with young girls. Paper Doll, ca. 1920. From Minnesota Historical Society. Rights: Attribution-ShareAlike 2.0 Generic. Courtesy: Flickr.com

Audrey Schwartzenburg Maduell

My parents, Frederick Schwartzenburg and Mildred Falk, married in 1919 and lived with my grandparents, Gustave and Maggie Falk, in a rented house on West End Boulevard and Howard Avenue, which is now Florida Avenue. This was the outskirts of New Orleans, later to be called Lakeview. They liked Lakeview so much that both parents and grandparents bought property on the corner of Pontchartrain Boulevard and Stafford Place. This was a weeded area, which was developed by Stafford, Derbes and Roy. The streets coming off of Pontchartrain Boulevard are named after them and go from Pontchartrain Boulevard to the Avenue C canal, now called Fleur de Lis Avenue. While waiting for the house to be built, the Schwartzenburgs lived on Canal Street near Broad Street, where my brother, Fred Jr., was born on January 17, 1923. My grandparents, the Falks, moved into their new home at 115 Stafford Place in January 1924. Shortly after that, my parents moved into 8400 Pontchartrain Boulevard and the address is now 6932. I was born January 4, 1925, making me the same age as the house. Our house was built to be a double Spanish-style shotgun, but it appeared to be a single because one front door faced Pontchartrain Boulevard. The other front door faced Stafford Place. My grandparents later converted their house into a double. Both houses had front and back screen porches to protect from mosquitos and catch the breezes from Lake Pontchartrain.

Our new neighbors, the Stecklers, the Talens, and the Dunns, became very close friends with us. There were also some bootleggers who moved into the neighborhood and whose house got raided before we got to know them. Over on Hay Place lived more friends named the Loyacanos and the Boudreauxs. A block or two north of our house is where Pontchartrain Boulevard ended. The cross street was Old Hammond Highway, which crossed the 17th Street Canal and took you into an area called Bucktown, which was a small fishing village.

The whole area from Pontchartrain Boulevard to the 17th Street Canal and from Old Hammond Highway to the railroad tracks and Metairie Cemetery was a large cypress swamp. The developers, Stafford, Derbes, and Roy, somehow negotiated to get it drained, and a few raised houses were built. Pontchartrain Boulevard was a raised shell road running along the west side of the New Basin Canal, and we called it the Shell Road. This New

Basin Canal was a very important waterway. It began at Lake Pontchartrain and ended somewhere downtown near Howard Avenue in central New Orleans. Much produce from the north shore of the lake was carried into New Orleans by barges traveling the canal. It was hand dug by Irish immigrants who worked for one dollar a day and many of whom died of yellow fever after having been bitten by the mosquitos from the swamp. Today the canal is filled and there exists a large green area between West End Boulevard and Pontchartrain Boulevard. Somewhere near 40th Street there is a large Celtic cross on this green space surrounded by large marble blocks found when filling the area. These were used to line the sides of the canal. The cross is a memorial dedicated to the hard working Irishmen who perished while working on this canal.

There were bridges crossing the New Basin Canal. There was the Lakeview Bridge crossing at Metairie Road, then the railroad bridge crossing Greenwood Cemetery, better known as the Black Bridge, and finally, the Marina Channel, which was the only bridge on Pontchartrain Boulevard. This connected West End Boulevard to West End Park and to the Southern Yacht Club. There were locks across the canal by Masson's Restaurant, which had previously been the Chez Paree night club. Late at night, we could hear the music carried by the breeze from the lake. Around West End Park, there were many seafood restaurants. Among them were Fitzgerald's, Bruning's and many more, all of which were washed away by Hurricane Katrina. Near and between these seafood restaurants were various nightclubs, like the popular Louis Prima Club where Louis Armstrong sometimes appeared. Also, there was the My Oh My Club with its female impersonators. Then, as mentioned before, there was the Southern Yacht Club, which was one of the oldest in the nation, and which sponsored regatta races. Presently, it is being rebuilt after a fire following Katrina.

West End Park, where all of the above attractions were, was entered by two bridges. One bridge was built at the end of Pontchartrain Boulevard crossing the channel entrance to the Marina. The other was a wooden car/pedestrian bridge crossing the 17th Street Canal from Bucktown. West End Park was a beautiful, small park, which drew crowds of people who came to see a wonderful water show at the round fountain in the center of the park. This was a raised structure with a room underneath for the operator to control the height of the spurts of water and the changing colored lights. People sat on benches surrounding this fountain enjoying the free show on warm summer nights. Sometimes when the wind blew in your direction you got soaked with water. There was a small wading pool surrounding the fountain where kids could play in the day time. Along the paved sidewalk around West End Park, there were swings and picnic tables and small shelters, which made it ideal for picnics and watermelon parties. Let me be sure to mention that this was the only place where kids could learn to skate or ride bikes because Lakeview had no sidewalks in the '30s.

On the lake side of West End Park, there was a fancy concrete wall, some of which still is there today. On the north side of Robert E. Lee Boulevard, there was the shore of Lake Pontchartrain. Many walkways were built over the water to reach the camps extending out into the lake. The West End street car and West End Boulevard ended at Robert E. Lee Boulevard. However, there was a small road continuing West End Boulevard to get to the lighthouse, which guided boats into the New Basin Canal. Beginning at the lighthouse, there was a long seawall made of concrete steps, which was built in the '30s and extended along the shore of Lake Pontchartrain all the way to the Industrial Canal. Close to the lighthouse was a small sandy beach, which was a fun play spot for kids to swim in the clear, clean water. The lighthouse was blown half way into the water during Hurricane Katrina. It is presently being rebuilt and is used as a maritime museum.

The area between the seawall and Robert E. Lee Boulevard was filled with shells and sand. The camps were demolished in the '30s and '40s and Laguard Army Hospital was built as a temporary hospital for returning soldiers. The area between Canal Boulevard and Bayou St. John likewise was filled and a temporary Navy and Coast Guard hospital was built. Today that same land is a beautiful part of Lakeview called Lakeshore East and Lakeshore West.

My memory goes back to the seawall, where my dad, on his way to work, placed a lantern on a step to hold a spot for the evening. This was when he would catch shrimp, crabs or fish, and enjoy socializing with many people who spent the evening hours relaxing with families along the shore.

Since we lived on Pontchartrain Boulevard, which was a road on the west side of the New Basin Canal, you might say this canal was our summertime playground. My dad built a wharf on the canal by our house and here is where I learned to swim. After instructions, he tied a rope around my waist and threw me in. My mother came later to check my progress and was proud of me until I rose out of the water without the rope. She was shocked but happy that I managed to swim so fast. Beverly Steckler, while swimming with us, disappeared, and luckily her hair touched my brother Fred's feet, and he rescued her, the hero! We had an old skiff, which leaked. Sometimes we managed to get it into the middle of the canal, and then it would start to sink. The people in the street car always got a big laugh from our antics. Many times we swam across the canal and climbed aboard the luxury yachts like the Ruth, the Port Bon Air, or the Bon Secuire, which were anchored across from our wharf, and we would pretend that we were on a cruise.

A few blocks up Pontchartrain Boulevard, my grandfather owned the Gus Falk Pan Am service station. He not only serviced the few cars on Pontchartrain Boulevard, but over the levee he serviced boats from his wharf. He also used the wharf to drop crab nets. One day he had his picture in the newspaper, showing the largest crab ever caught in the New Basin Canal.

We raised all kinds of animals. Some were for Sunday dinner, like chickens, ducks and turkeys and even a goat. My dad also sold Virginia Life Insurance, and one customer gave him a monkey because he became a nuisance by tearing her clothes. Needless to say, the monkey gave us a lot of fun, but became a problem for us also.

I have wonderful memories of a country-type life living among a few houses and amidst vacant land filled with woods. We spent many hours picking blackberries, so that Mother could bake pies for us. One day, we kids went exploring deeper and deeper into the woods until it became dark, and it took a while before we found a path back to the houses. Our parents were frantic and furious, so we were all punished. We had a few encounters with snakes in the area also. I picked up something that looked like a rope one day, only to find it crawled off when I let it go.

There was a vacant lot across Stafford Place, which my parents cleared and planted a few veggies on. My grandpa planted dwarf okra, which grew to be seven feet tall. Our tenant planted eggplant, which were beautiful and plump. When he tried to cut into them, he could not. The boys shot matchsticks into them when they were young and skin grew over them. We also had banana trees. The fruit was small but good. Our monkey, Johnny, really liked them.

When the area became populated, my dad bought the lot across Stafford Place so that my mom could continue to hang her clothes out to dry.

Life was simple and fun. When we needed shoes and clothes, my mother took us downtown on the West End street car. My brother's idea of a treat was to buy a bag of nails to build things around the house. Every weekend my brother helped my dad work on our Model A or Model T Ford while I stayed busy playing with friends around that corner of Pontchartrain Boulevard and Stafford Place. Actually, the street was narrow and made of shells with ditches on each side of the street. At the entrance, there was a big concrete and stucco arch with the words "Stafford Place" in lights. We had foot races and bike races ending at a string tied to each side of the arch. My friend, Kitty Steckler, and I ran around the columns, jumping over the string until I missed, cutting my knee. Believe me, there is nothing like a knee cut on shells. I'll bet every kid in Lakeview can remember cuts on shells mainly because there were no paved streets.

Lakeview School, which is still on Milne Street, although empty and falling apart, holds special memories for me. I could mention favorite teachers and friends I made whom I still keep in touch with. These were Mary Meek, Connie Hinkel and Muriel Bonie, all separated by Hurricane Katrina. The play yard for girls was on the lake side of the school. We played go in and out the window, London Bridge, a tisket—a tasket, and jump rope, and we always carried jacks and a ball to play on the basement floor on rainy days. Of course, I did not have much time to play at lunch due to the big lunches my mother made for this slow eater.

When I first started school, we were carpooled due to the fact that we were living on the west side of the New Basin Canal. Later, my parents and neighbors got together and hired Mr. Johnny Klein to drive us on his bus, which we called the West End bus. He traveled along Pontchartrain Boulevard, picking up kids all along the way and to get the Talen kids at Talen's flower nursery. Klein always tooted his horn when he passed our house so that I would be ready when he made his return trip. I could never finish breakfast in time. What a sight I was, running to catch the bus while my mother was helping me gulp milk.

Our principal, Miss Emma Betzer, was always there ringing her hand bell, waiting for the two school buses to arrive. She called the Spanish Fort Bus the Singing Kids bus and the Bucktown bus the Bloody Nose bus. The kids were so rough that Miss Betzer had to be ready to apply first-aid any morning.

While still attending Lakeview School, I began taking tumbling lessons from Mr. Eddie Reggio. One day he told me to bring my roller skates to class to learn to dance on skates. I didn't tell him I had none. After all, there were no paved sidewalks, so I rushed out to buy a pair and went to West End Park to learn in one try on the paved sidewalk around the park. At the studio, I wobbled all over the place. This was probably good, because I learned acrobatics on them. By the time I went to Sophie B. Wright High School, I became known for my acrobatics on skates. To this day, jokingly, classmates ask if I still dance on skates.

Some of our neighbor girls attended Hilda Torbio's Dance School in Lakeview. I cried until my mother gave me a quarter to take a class. That is how my dancing career began.

▲ The seawall along Lake Pontchartrain. In the 1930s it was made of concrete steps that extended into the water. Courtesy: Muriel B. MacHauer

Hilda excelled in tap, and at the first meeting for recital, my mother recognized my God-given talent. Mr. Kieffer, the father of daughter Joyce and son Louis, located a teacher named Dorothy Norris for classical ballet. The Kieffer kids and I all studied ballet and under Mr. Eddie Reggio, we studied acrobatics in Mr. Kieffer's basement on Polk Avenue. Louis Kieffer and I did a dance together at the Lakeview School May Festival. It was a Spanish dance called La Cumparsita. Our recitals were in the church at Polk Avenue and Catina Street.

When Dorothy Norris left New Orleans, I studied ballet and character dance with Lelia Haller. My training in tap was with the professional, Adelaide Lamar. I continued to become professional myself, dancing four years in the South and five years in New York City.

After World War II, I returned to my Lakeview home and family and married a Lakeview boy, a US Navy pilot named Louis Maduell. We raised our family in this beautiful part of New Orleans. While doing so, I opened my own school, which I named Our Lady of Grace Dancing School.

Having my home and contents destroyed by Katrina and leaving Lakeview was not my choice. I can only be grateful that most of the years of my life were spent here. It was the best place to live and to grow up, and my memories will last forever.

▼ The refurbished fountain in the center of West End Park. On Sunday nights in the 1920s and 30s a technician worked inside the small structure near the fountain, changing the lights and height of the various fountains of water while people sat around on benches to enjoy the show. Courtesy: Muriel B. MacHauer.

Louis Marion Maduell

I was born in 1919 when my folks lived on North Broad Street in New Orleans. I was named for the doctor who saved my mother's life and mine after a difficult delivery. My parents, Charles Rene Maduell and Louise Viosca Maduell, bought property in Lakeview, 5650 Ada Place, between Taylor Avenue, which is now Florida Avenue, and the Southern Illinois railroad tracks. The street is parallel to and one block east of Canal Boulevard. Ada Place was paved with clam shells and oyster shells, and the developer converted service alleys in order to fit in three streets named for his wife Ada and sons Charles and James. In 1919, my father built our house with cypress wood, because after World War I, there was a shortage of pine. With my brother, Duke, we moved in when I was ten months old. Siblings Floyd and Lucille came along later.

At that time, there were few streets in Lakeview. The whole area was considered country. There were many wooded areas and dairy farms and Italian truck farms and grassy areas. Wooden bridges crossed the many canals. The Orleans canal and Orleans Avenue, which we called Turtleback Road, was just to the east of our house and separated Lakeview from the undeveloped part of City Park. On the east side of the canal, there was Marconi Drive. Marconi was the inventor of the telegraph, and in this area of City Park near the pumping station, there was a 400-foot-tall telegraph wireless radio transmitting/receiving station called Tropical Radio Company.

Lakeview was bounded by the Orleans canal on the east, the New Basin Canal on the west, Lake Pontchartrain on the north, and City Park Avenue on the south. West Lakeview, between the New Basin and 17th Street canals, was developed after World War II.

Lakeview School was located on Milne Street, Brooks Street, and Polk Avenue. The street was narrow and covered with shells running alongside of the algae-filled Milne canal. There was no swimming, fishing or playing in this canal. My stay at Lakeview School was short. On my first day of kindergarten, at the age of four, I did not know where to go when the bell rang for lunch, so I walked home across Canal Boulevard to Ada Place where I lived. My mother became furious at the lack of supervision, allowing a four-year-old child to leave the school grounds. Not long after this, she enrolled me at Beauregard

▲ The Beauregard Public School. Beauregard Public School started as a Grammar school and is now a Junior High School. Courtesy: New Orleans Public Library.

Grammar School. Before leaving Lakeview School, I remember the routine each morning. All classes gathered in the basement to recite the Pledge of Allegiance and sing our national anthem. When the teacher at the piano played a march, we marched to our classrooms. I stood there unable to move. My head was hanging down and my arm was up next to a post. Finally, a teacher realized that my finger was stuck in an eye of a hook. They had to use lard to loosen my finger. Another thing that I remember about Lakeview School, and Beauregard School too, was the long, dark cloak rooms between classrooms. These were provided for students to hang coats and hats before entering the classroom. I remember them as a place to stand a kid who could not behave. They were long and dark.

Lakeview was a safe place to play outdoors as most of us did. There was very little traffic. We played baseball or football in the streets or cleared areas. During the 1929 depression, we had one bicycle to share among four kids, but we were happy. To play outdoors was fun. To stay indoors meant to work, and my parents had a lot of that for us. When my baby sister, Lucille, was born, the doctor recommended fresh milk, so my mother bought a cow. She also raised chickens, ducks, and turkeys.

I had only one pair of shoes for school and church, therefore, I went barefoot to take our cows in a field. My older brother, Duke, milked them until he went to college at

Louisiana State University. I inherited the job and drove them to Ruffin's Dairy to mate with their bull. This way a calf was born and we were assured of getting milk. I envied the Ruffin boys, Charlie and Peter, who rode horses, because we never owned a horse. They had one sister named Emma. Another dairy was located between Polk Avenue and Florida Avenue. It was owned by the Dideban family. These were large dairies selling their milk in many neighborhoods in New Orleans.

My mother also raised canaries and pedigreed collie dogs and won awards for prize turkeys and chickens. She had a large incubator in the backyard for hatching eggs, which she received from all over the American continent. I guess we had the city's first airplane landing strip right there on Canal Boulevard at the corner of Florida Avenue. A few barnstormers tied their planes to large billboards there after selling rides to people interested in seeing the city from the air. At night, I and some neighbor kids climbed in them and pretended we were pilots. I was eight years old then and I wanted to fly. I did so when later I became a Navy aviator.

Some fun things we did while growing up were that we caught a small owlet that we named Who. We told my dad Who was in our garage, and he answered, "I don't know," and that went on until we released it and were surprised when the owl returned to say goodbye.

My mom taught us many chores. We all learned to cook, wash dishes and clothes, and clean house. We learned to use hand tools and built sheds and fences. When it was time to build a front porch, we sent Mom off so she couldn't order us around.

My mom took me out of Lakeview School because of lack of supervision by the teachers. I attended Beauregard Elementary School on Canal Street across from St. Anthony Church. After that, I attended Jesuit High School on a football scholarship. I ran track at City Park's Tad Gormley Stadium where I now have a seat named in my honor. I always worked during my school years, delivering groceries on my bike and delivering milk and eggs for my mom. In the evenings, I sold *Saturday Evening Post* magazines to couples in the parking lots behind Rockery Inn and Lenfant's Restaurant.

After my 1938 Jesuit graduation, I attended LSU and worked at E.B. Ludwig Steel Construction Company and many other places. Later I joined the US Navy and became a naval aviation cadet at the US Naval Air Station on the New Orleans lakefront. Afterwards, I was sent for eight months of training at Corpus Christi, Texas, and became an ensign. I loved the Navy and flying. And after World War II, I stayed in the US Navy Reserves with two active duty tours. I retired as a lieutenant commander. During the war, I was in three theaters of action. They were the Caribbean Sea, the Aleutian Islands, and the Mediterranean Sea. After the war, I was transferred to the Navy Reserve Squadron at the New Orleans lakefront.

When I re-entered the Navy on active duty, I became an operations officer. I met Audrey Schwartzenburg, aprofessional ballet/acrobatic dancer who was home from a tour of dancing in New York City.

My mother knew Audrey during her days working as a chaperone with the USO. This organization took groups of girls to dances at the nearby military bases around New Orleans. She introduced me to Miss Audrey, and within ten minutes I knew I had found my wife. A year later we were married and being in the military, moved around the country as our five children were born.

By 1959, we returned to Lakeview and bought a home to finish raising our family. As stated before, West Lakeview was developed after World War II. Our last home was at 338 Twelfth Street, which is now a shell due to Hurricane Katrina. It was sold to the Road Home and holds many happy memories. Life in Lakeview was good from the beginning of our lives until 2005. As we all know, Hurricane Katrina changed it all. We now live in Mandeville on the Northshore. Our grown children are near and thankful to God that we have all survived. I and my family have happy memories of growing up in Lakeview.

▲ Louis Maduell as a child. Courtesy: Maduell family.

▲ The flying field used by Jimmy Wedell in the 1920s at Canal and Harrison. Photo by Edward. E. Agnelly. Courtesy: Tulane University

JOYCE KIEFFER MOHR

I was born to parents Alga Piton and John Kieffer in 1928. Some time before I was five, my parents, together with me and my older brother Louis, moved into Lakeview and lived on Polk Avenue. Later they sold this house and moved into a house in the 6400 block of Milne Street. At that time, there was a canal running down the middle of Milne Street. It was not an attractive canal for catching minnows as it was always filled with green algae. After a while, we moved to a nice house with a big backyard at the corner of Wuerpel and Lane streets where I finished growing up.

Louis attended Lakeview School while I attended St. Dominic School. Louis and I loved our tumbling lessons, which we took from Mr. Reggio. He taught private lessons in acrobatics and tumbling. Louis was truly the athletic type and stayed fit even into his adult life by running marathons. Mr. Reggio taught many kids in the area, including one of our friends, Audrey Schwartzenburg, also from Lakeview School. Every year when Lakeview School held their May festival, Louis and Audrey did an acrobatic routine. One year he and Audrey did a Spanish dance together. They were the hit of Mr. Reggio's class. Louis joined the US Navy during World War II, and after that he married and left Lakeview to live in the Lower Garden District of New Orleans on Annunciation Square, where he and his wife raised three children. He continued staying fit and many years later died after walking a marathon.

I stayed at St. Dominic School until I finished seventh grade. It was there that I made some lifelong friends, some of whom I still meet. The school was small. There were only five or six girls in our class. There was Edna Mae Pedeaux, Genevieve Monahan, Rae Ann Richards and Loraine Prudhomme. I remember that all of our teachers were nuns and my favorite was Sister Josepha.

My parents had one auto. At that time, we were living through the Great Depression. Finally, in 1951, they bought a car, which my mother drove. My dad never learned to drive. We went everywhere riding the street cars. The good old West End street car ran on tracks along the bank of the New Basin Canal. My mother, like most ladies in the neighborhood, bought all groceries from the corner grocery store. There were quite a few in Lakeview at the time. Our favorite summertime refreshments were five-cents snow balls from Mr. Pete's snowball stand on West End Boulevard. He had no electric machine to grind the ice. He used a hand grinder and filled the ice with the most delicious syrup in the world.

For entertainment, I played games with my friends. There was always a ball game in vacant lots, or we played board games and paper dolls on screened porches. Nearly every house had a screened porch, which was the family living room during the hot summer days and nights when the mosquitos came out to feast. Let us not forget the good old window fan before air conditioning or central heating even existed.

My high school education was at McMain High School, the uptown girls high school. It took about five transfers from street car to public service bus, to another street car and so on to get there for only seven cents. A person could ride all over town for just seven cents and also get a free ride on the Canal Street ferry to Algiers and back again. After I graduated from McMain High School, I went to work in an accounting office for Southern Bell and Telephone Company.

The boy I married was also from Lakeview and attended Lakeview School, but we did not meet until we were grown. Richard Mohr was too young to serve in World War II, but he joined the reserves. We married in 1949 and stayed in Lakeview where we raised two sons and one daughter, who were born in 1951, 1953, and 1955. One of my sons lives in River Ridge with his family and the other, who never married, loves old New Orleans and lives in the Garden District. My daughter and her family of three children live in Lacombe.

My parents' home on the corner of Wuerpel and Lane streets was sold several times over the years and survived Hurricane Katrina. The present owners have turned it into a beautiful show piece by adding on and remodeling.

I have so many lingering memories of this home and my childhood days here in Lakeview. I too have survived Katrina and am still enjoying my present home and all the fond memories of a happy life growing up right here where I belong.

Ora Dedebant Mollere

My parents had their first dairy in Lakeview on land near City Park and near the pumping station, which is located over the Orleans canal and the railroad tracks at the end of Florida Avenue. It was one of the largest dairies in Lakeview. There was a lot of vacant land. In fact, there were no streets cut through between Florida Avenue and Harrison Avenue. Later, they moved and rented a home. It was on the 6300 block of General Haig Street. The dairy was moved also and next to our dairy was a house owned by the Suguette family, and much later it was owned by the Mollere family. General Haig Street was not cut through all the way to Filmore Avenue, so there was a lot of land for the cows to graze. From Filmore Avenue to Robert E. Lee Boulevard, General Haig Street was made of shells with gutters on each side, and a few homes were built there.

I was born after the move to General Haig Street. I was the baby of the family. I had one brother named Johnny and two sisters named Rosalie and Margaret. I have memories of my uncles driving the cows up the shell street of General Haig and keeping them away from the few houses with nice front lawns. They brought them to graze out by Lake Pontchartrain. I sometimes walked behind them, but when it was time to return home, I would get tired, so they sat me up on a cow to ride home.

On Harrison Avenue, there were a few stores and houses. I made friends with the children there. I remember the Virgadamo girls and Mary and Gerry Quaid. Their daddy built a small playground next to their house with swings and a slide and seesaw. He built a sign that read "Mary and Gerry Playground."

When it was time for me to attend school, I attended Lakeview Public School for kindergarten and later I attended St. Dominic Catholic School on Harrison Avenue. By the time I was nine, my parents moved the dairy and built their home out by the causeway near Lake Pontchartrain. I attended third grade at St. Francis Catholic School until I graduated. Then I went on to McDonogh High School. My years living in Lakeview were not very long, but they were happy years.

My grandparents were perhaps early settlers because I remember my parents telling me about grandfather owning an island in City Park in 1900. During a terrible storm and flood, the island was completely lost and there remains no record of it.

In 1946, Roland Mollere and I married and have made Metairie home ever since. Roland and I raised four beautiful children. And in 1980, we opened our own restaurant, which we named R & O's Restaurant.

Lakeview was a very good place for children to grow up. There was City Park and its many attractions and swimming in clean Lake Pontchartrain out by the West End lighthouse and enjoying the beach at Spanish Fort. Our parents were hard working people who managed to survive the Great Depression and keep their families together. They also kept Lakeview a clean, good suburb and the attractive place it is today.

▼ Gentilly Terrace section of New Orleans, Louisiana in 1922. Undeveloped land used as cow pasture By Percy Viosca, Jr.. (Percy Viosca, Jr.. photograph) Rights: Public domain.
Courtesy: Wikimedia Commons

Connie Hinkel Negrotto

My parents, Ralph and Inez Hinkel, moved into Lakeview when I was five. They bought a house at 5771 Ridgeway Place on the corner of Kenilworth Street in 1929. I and my younger brother, Ray, grew up in this happy neighborhood. I remember the house, which was off of the ground on piers, as all houses were built in case of heavy rain or flood. There was a screened porch across the front and also one across the back of our house, and each porch had a swing for us to enjoy and relax and catch the breeze. This was where we spent our summers playing games when we weren't outside under the oak tree in our backyard. I loved playing ladies and dressing up in my mother's discarded clothes and high heels with my girlfriends and cousins, June and Joyce. My brother and his friends joined us along with my neighbor, Mildred Muller. We played hide-and-seek, marbles, jacks and gave penny parties, to name a few. Most houses had screened porches to avoid heat, rain, or mosquitos. In the wintertime, we kept warm with small gas heaters or open fireplaces.

Since my dad was a chief engineer on ships, he was not home most of the time while we were growing up. When he was home, however, he tried to care for the house and yard. Being an engineer, he had some idea that there was a pocket of gas below his property. He decided on a spot in our backyard to carry out his experiment. The only equipment that he had was a garden hose, a barrel of gravel, rocks, and a long pipe. He softened the ground with water from the hose to drive the pipe into the ground. He used the weight of the barrel of gravel to drive the pipe down. The barrel was attached by chains to a high scaffold. Eventually, after several lengths of pipe, he struck gas and capped it and attached a line to our kitchen stove. This was used for a while until the vein ran out. This made the news all around Lakeview, and being a child, I never learned the details of this episode. My dad passed away in January 1959. My mother lived in this house until 1962 when the highway system began building the Interstate 610 and the expressway to downtown New Orleans. All of this property in Lakeview was bought from the owners, thereby moving many people. By 1962, West Lakeview was developed and my mother built a house, and we all moved there.

Our house on Ridgeway Place was near Lakeview School, therefore, I walked to school back and forth each day and even coming home for lunch. My memories of our principal,

Miss Betzer, were that she was very strict. She used a brass hand bell to call us in each morning where we lined up in the basement to pledge allegiance to our flag, and she rang her bell once more to signal us to march upstairs to our classrooms while Miss Pecararo, our music appreciation teacher, played a march on the piano. The same bell rang at 3 p.m. to dismiss us. There was no PA system in those days.

Our school held a spring festival each year, at which time each class had a turn to dress up and do a dance together. Our parents organized and bought from the many booths selling refreshments and from the "white elephant" booth selling donated items.

There were a few businesses across from and near the school, namely Mr. Joe's shoe repair shop, Mr. Everett's pharmacy, Miss Singletary's grocery— where we sometimes went to get French bread sandwiches and a jumbo bottle of pop for five cents—and Mr. Minton's barber shop where my brother and dad always had their hair cut.

Around the corner from our house was a grocery store named Rosemary's, where my mother sent my brother Ray and I to buy groceries. We would take our little red wagon, and we were given each a penny to buy candy, and believe me we got a lot of lagniappe with that. Families had to buy groceries daily because we did not have a freezer in the '30s. We had an ice box and a delivery man who sold ice once or twice a week.

One of my close friends from Lakeview School was Muriel, who lived far out on General Haig Street and rode the Spanish Fort bus. Another close friend was Audrey, who lived on Pontchartrain Boulevard across the New Basin Canal and rode the Bucktown bus. Another close friend was Mary who lived on Milne Street near my house. To get to visit Muriel, I rode my balloon tire bike over a mile to spend the day playing house in her little playhouse in the backyard.

Although not within the bounds of Lakeview, we considered beautiful City Park a place for all ages to relax, picnic and have fun under the magnificent oak trees. There was the kiddie pool, the big swimming pool, the tennis courts, the paddle boats, swings, slides and a merry-go-round, which we called flying horses. Let us not forget the little train that took us for a ride around the park.

The Peristyle was a place to hold parties and have entertainment. We liked having our picture taken on the concrete lions, which were placed beside the steps, and in the lagoon's swans and ducks swam by. On Sunday afternoon, my cousins, June and Joyce, and our parents walked to City Park to be entertained at the bandstand across from the casino. Usually a dancing school performed, and the police band played while we enjoyed ice cream or popcorn, which was sold at the casino. We walked back home at night with my mother and aunt and my two girl cousins never having fear of any problems along the way. It was summertime and always someone was sitting on their porch in the dark trying to keep cool. Lights on a porch would only attract bugs and mosquitos.

Another favorite place of mine was the Delgado Museum that is now the New Orleans Museum of Art. I enjoyed a visit there to see the many works of art, sculpture, and artifacts.

As I grew old enough to go on dates, a favorite place to dance and have refreshments was Lenfant's on Canal Boulevard. The juke box played all of our favorite music, and the dance floor was always crowded. It was a real teen hangout. Smoochers parked their cars in the parking lot behind the building and were served food and drinks by car hops, who hooked a serving tray onto the rolled down window of the car. Remember, no air-conditioning in cars back then.

We lived close to the New Basin Canal and boarded the West End street car to downtown at the cost of seven cents. We waited for the car on a platform that extended out over the water. I remember how the car would rock from side to side when the motorman gave it full speed after making the turn at City Park Avenue and headed to Lake Pontchartrain. My dad took us for a ride on this street car when he went crabbing. He would take his basket, scoop net, crab nets, and bait, and my brother, Ray, and I would go to Lake Pontchartrain and catch blue crabs. What a treat when my mother boiled those crabs for our feast.

St. Dominic Church was a small brick building located on the corner of Harrison Avenue and Milne Street. Since we were Catholic, we attended Mass on Sundays and High Holy days walking eight blocks each way. I also attended catechism classes and joined the choir and the Blessed Virgin Mary Sodality. Father Paretti was our priest then, and every spring there was a festival held in the playground area. Our sodality always helped at the candy booth.

So much of Lakeview has changed since the '30s and '40s. I was fortunate to have a happy childhood there. And although I moved temporarily, most of my life has been spent in the beautiful part of New Orleans. I lived through World War II and married my neighbor, Allen J. Negrotto, and returned to West Lakeview to raise our two daughters on Bellaire Drive. Allen served in the US Navy Air Force. Years passed, and I continued to enjoy my home in Lakeview until the flood after Hurricane Katrina snatched it away from me. I sold the flood damaged house to others to repair and enjoy it, but the memory will always belong to me

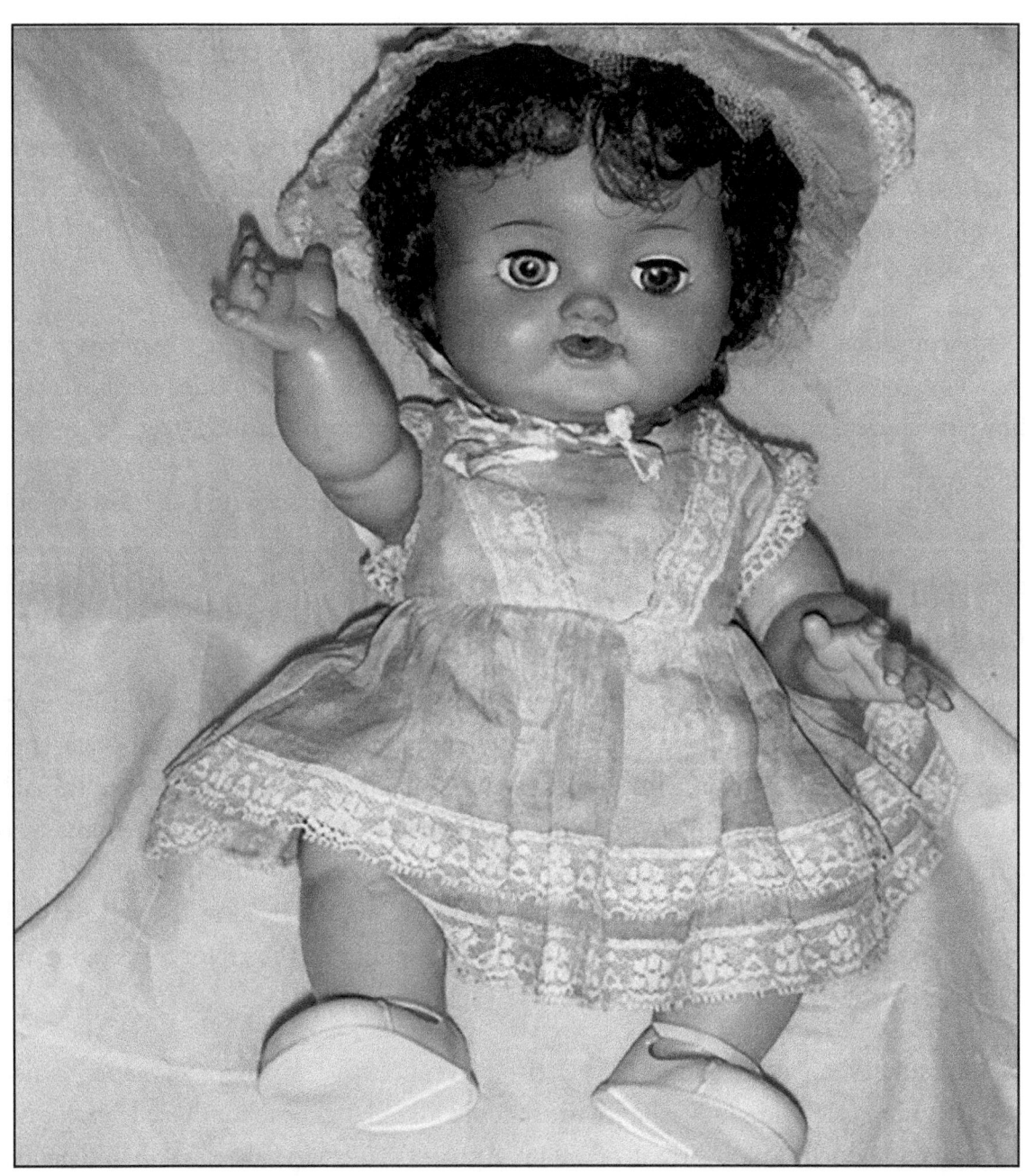

▲ Every little girl wanted a doll that said "Mama". Photo by Cathy Adams. Courtesy: RubyLane.com

ARMAND PEYROUX

My dad, Armand Peyroux, and my mother, Anita Delaune Peyroux, built a house in Lakeview on the corner of Germaine and Milne streets in or about the year 1925. They moved into the house with their three little girls, Alice, Gloria, and Audrey. I was born later in 1929.

My education started in kindergarten at St. Dominic School where my oldest sisters attended. Alice, the oldest, attended Mount Carmel Academy. St. Dominic had classrooms above the church, which faced Harrison Avenue at the corner of Catina Street.

I stayed at St. Dominic School until the fifth grade and then went to Lakeview School, which was the only public school in Lakeview. I had many friends from both schools, some of whom I still remember. There was Bob Sanderson, Norbert Delph, and Claude Spies, to name a few.

Being from a good Catholic family, we were very close to our church. My dad was an usher and I was an altar boy for several years when Father Paretti was pastor. Everyone loved him with his Spanish accent. He was such a caring priest. He always visited the sick in the parish along with his many other duties. Our teachers were Carmelite nuns who were also very good to us. They lived in a small wooden house behind the church facing Catina Street. Later, Father Lopey came to our parish, and he lived in the rectory with Father Paretti across the parking lot next to the brick church. The rectory was along the Milne canal.

Across the Milne canal and facing Harrison Avenue was a small grocery store owned by Mr. Gordon. He sold sandwiches to the school kids at lunchtime for those who did not walk home for lunch. Like nearly all of the small grocery stores in Lakeview, he sold people their supplies on credit. At this time, we were living through the Great Depression of 1929. So many people had to pay at the end of the week because so many were out of work. My parents were extremely lucky because my dad worked in the post office and had a steady job. Many of my friends had far less than we had, but it made no difference to kids. We were all happy growing up together.

I had relatives living close by and we felt welcome in anyone's kitchen when the cooking aroma was inviting. My Aunt Rose and Uncle Henry McCoy lived a half block away on Catina Street. Their two daughters were Beverly and Rosemary, who were very close cousins and always outside playing with us and the other neighbors. There was also my cousin, Jean Marie Couget, who was a champion swimmer. He would dive off of the Black Bridge over the New Basin Canal and Mound Avenue and swim all the way to the locks at the end where the canal met Lake Pontchartrain.

Needless to say, the New Basin Canal was the one and only favorite swimming spot for most kids in that part of Lakeview. Once in a while, my parents drove us to the sandy beach of Lake Pontchartrain where Bayou St. John entered the lake. There was an old fort there called Spanish Fort, and there was an amusement park there where we had rides like a ferris wheel and carousel, known in those days as flying horses. But getting back to the swimmers in the New Basin Canal, our fun was to swim out to the barges filled with watermelons and other produce from farms on the north shore of the lake to sell in downtown New Orleans. Once in a while, the workmen would throw us a watermelon, and we had a nice cool feast of ripe watermelon. The New Basin water was clean and clear in those days, and some people dropped crab nets from the street car shelters and caught big, blue crabs for cooking. The crabs never bothered the swimmers. I guess they knew to stay clear of us, and we stayed clear of them.

Lakeview was so different in those days. There were more trees and weeds and bushes than there were houses. One of our favorite pastimes was picking blackberries. There were wild blackberry bushes everywhere. In the summer, when they were ripe, we gathered blackberries, and we'd always carry a big stick to ward off snakes. Our mothers would bake blackberry pies. Oh, so delicious! Some families used vacant lots next to their houses to grow small vegetable gardens. Some people fenced in areas to raise chickens and ducks for cooking. Seafood was always free for the catching. Even though there was a depression, people did not starve.

There is one memory about the Milne canal that I will never forget. My dad built a wooden bridge across the canal in order to carry supplies when he built our house. It was a footbridge and everyone used it. On summer nights, the kids played outdoor games, chasing one another and hiding out. I was among the youngest and smallest of the children when a big game was in progress. My mother had just given me a bath and dressed me in clean clothes, but I wanted to join the rest of the kids by the bridge. Soon I slipped and fell into the dirty, filthy canal. Needless to say, my mother had a fit trying to get me cleaned up all over again.

After I graduated from Lakeview School in seventh grade, I went to the all-boys St. Aloysius High School and then to Warren Easton High School for boys. When I graduated from there at age seventeen, I joined the US Navy Reserves. After my tour of duty, I worked for the Whitney Bank, then the NBC Bank, and my final job was at the US Post Office, from which I am retired.

I married Flora at age thirty-four and left Lakeview and lived in Metairie for forty-one years. My memories of the beginnings of Lakeview will live with me forever, as will my happy childhood and the lasting friends I had growing up together in a time so long ago.

◀ The old Milneburg/Port Pontchartrain lighthouse with the bath houses and beach area shown. Uncredited WPA photographer, public domain. Courtesy: Wiki Commons

▼ Warren Easton High School. Courtesy: New Orleans Pubic Library

MARIE VIRGADAMO PORROVECCHIO

Since I am the youngest child of Antonio and Frances Virgadamo, I was born ten years after my sister, Frances, better known as Honey. That was 1931, and we lived on Memphis Street in the house my daddy built. I too helped my parents with many household chores, and I had many cousins and playmates nearby. There were few houses nearby and much vacant land giving the feeling of country living.

I started Lakeview School and stayed through seventh grade. At that time, there were no middle schools. From seventh grade we went directly to high school. We walked to Lakeview School because to be picked up by the school bus, you had to live on the north side of Harrison Avenue. The bus came from picking up kids by Spanish Fort and the last stop before Lakeview School was by my Aunt Lena's grocery store on the corner of Harrison Avenue and Memphis Street. We thought nothing of walking, since we walked everywhere. We had happy times walking to school or to St. Dominic Church on the corner of Harrison Avenue and Milne Street. We also went to catechism lessons taught by the nuns in the little gray hall behind the church. At that time, St. Dominic Church was located near two canals, the Harrison and the Milne canals. We walked on the gravel street, not near the canal because it was slippery and we did not want to fall in where the crawfish lived.

I had a happy childhood living in Lakeview. There were no luxuries like air conditioning and TVs and the long list of entertainments that kids can't live without today. Our parents made the best of the terrible depression where everyone had to struggle to keep the family fed. Of course, the comforts were not yet invented, but we were raised with love and family togetherness. We were happy with what we had.

When in school, I loved sports and ran track at Lakeview School. Then at John McDonogh High School, I excelled in gym. When I left high school, I continued my education at South Western Business College. Then during World War II, I worked as a secretary. And by 1951, I met and married Tom, a local boy. We lived in apartments on Rampart Street, then on Clouet Street and then on France Street, where my son was born. By 1964, we were happy to find our own home on the corner of Hay Place and Fleur de Lis in good old Lakeview. It is here I raised my son and two daughters.

As all from Lakeview know, we were very near the 17th Street Canal where the levee broke and flooded our home and the entire area. We lost our beautiful home but fortunately not our lives to Hurricane Katrina. I have rebuilt my home in the same location where I still live. My love for Lakeview continues.

▲ Every little girl wanted a Betsy Wetsy Doll. Photo by Cathy Adams. Courtesy: RubyLane.com

PAT REILLY REBENNE

My father, Harry Reilly, was born in 1902. In 1904 his father died. And in 1906 his mother died, leaving six children. The children were split between their grandmother Finley and their Uncle Pat Reilly. Their next-door neighbor on South Dupre Street in New Orleans was moving to Lakeview for cheaper rent, and since their son, Roy, was the same age as my father, they offered to take my father and raise him even though they had four children of their own. So, my father from his earliest memories grew up at the lake and remained living there until 1929 when he married my mother and then moved to 3012 Tulane Avenue where I was born in 1930. Andrew Miller was a baker and was the bridge tender over the New Basin Canal at the end of the street car line on West End Boulevard. Louise Miller was a wonderful, bubbly grandmother-type person and so was my Grandmother Miller. They moved around at the lake quite a bit, always for cheaper rent and a better house. My father joked about coming home some night and found that they had moved during the day. There were no sidewalks or roads back then where we lived, and my father told how he would wade through swamp and muck from the street car to the house. As was the custom in the 1930s, family visited family, and my earliest recollection is riding the street car on the trestle on West End Boulevard to the lake on Sunday after church. I recall several houses they lived in. One was on Pontchartrain Boulevard, probably close to what is now Filmore Avenue. One was on Regent Street and Robert E. Lee Boulevard, behind what was then the Beach House and was later Masson's Restaurant. There was one more on Old Hammond Highway and one on the road leading back to West End Park. The one on Pontchartrain Boulevard was in the 8500 block, which is about where the Pontchartrain Point restaurant is today. They always had chickens and ducks in the yard, and Mrs. Miller put on a good Sunday dinner with fresh baked bread. I can smell it yet. I remember their dog, whose name was Blizzard. I used to sit on his back like he was a pony. After dinner, we walked to Bruning's Restaurant and Joe Lenfant's, where my father visited with his buddies and with whom he grew up and probably had a beer or two. Then we went home on the street car, and boy, did that car rock on the trestle along the New Basin Canal. This was our ritual until the 1940s when the Millers died.

A few years later, I married, and we moved to Lakeview where we lived for forty years. My father used to comment on the difference he saw in 1960 from when he moved to Lakeview in 1906. This is the Lakeview I knew and loved.

▲ New Orleans Street Cars, Past & Present. All streetcars were green and the West End Streetcar line (pictured to the right above) were the most memorable to Lakeview residents. Streetcar on St. Charles across from Tulane (2761126390)" by Tulane Public Relations - streetcar on St. Charles across from Tulane Uploaded by Albert Herring. Licensed under CC BY 2.0 Courtesy: Wikimedia Commons

Gerrie Quaid Rodrigue

When I think back on my childhood growing up in Lakeview, my memories are mostly happy ones. I was extremely fortunate to be born to a loving, caring family. My parents settled into their large basement house sometime before 1924. It truly was the largest house on General Haig Street. It was located at 6655 General Haig Street, just a few lots on the south side of Filmore Avenue. From Filmore Avenue all the way to Harrison Avenue, there were no streets. It was all vacant land. This was pasture land for the cows owned by the Debedon family, who operated their dairy near Harrison Avenue.

My parents were Michael Quaid and Julie Brechtel. They had seven children. I was the second-to-last child. There were Harry, Cecile, Catherine, Patricia, Robert—"Buddy"—then me, and last of all, Mary.

When I was four, my mother died delivering Mary, so many family members lived with us, and we were lovingly cared for by all of them. My father, who was a fireman with the New Orleans Fire Department, died four years after my mother. They say that he died of pneumonia or of grief. The house remained full. We were cared for by aunts and uncles. Living with us also were my oldest brother, Harry, and his wife, Sue. My Aunt Bernie O'Brian also came from Texas to stay and care for us. She had the only car in the family, so she drove us to St. Dominic School and managed our education. My Aunt Bessie, better known as Mrs. West, and my uncle lived nearby and took care of the house and had a small grocery in the basement. She sold a few items like milk, bread, and candy to the few neighbors from around. They had one son, Tom, who was assistant fire chief with the New Orleans Fire Department. Martha was a grown cousin who came to live with us and took care of the girls in our family. She saw to it that our hair was always pretty with ribbons and curls and kept us well dressed. She was a beautician who worked downtown and took the Robert E. Lee bus and the West End street car every morning and evening to get to and from work. The street car had cane seats and ran from West End Boulevard by the New Basin Canal to Spanish Fort at Bayou St. John. The motorman usually dropped crab nets in the bayou and checked them at the end of the line so he could carry his crabs home for supper at the end of the day. My aunt walked on General Haig Street, which was covered with shells, a few blocks to wait for the little Robert E. Lee Bus and then transferred to the

West End street car at the end of West End Boulevard. She then traveled all the way along the New Basin Canal to finally get to Canal Street, which was the main business area of New Orleans.

My dad and the rest of the men in my family built a small playground next to our big house. There were swings and a slide and a see-saw. They painted a sign titled "Gerrie and Mary Playground," and a few kids in our neighborhood were welcome. There was always something to amuse us like picking blackberries, jumping rope or playing jacks. Sometimes my Aunt Bernie drove us to the amusement park by Spanish Fort to ride the rides or play on the small sandy beach by Lake Pontchartrain. There was also a small beach by the lighthouse at the end of the New Basin Canal and West End Boulevard where we enjoyed swimming.

My education began at St. Dominic School, where I made many friends and finished the seventh grade. Then I attended Mount Carmel Academy, also in Lakeview, where I did very well. One of my many friends was Mary L. Windmer, who is now a writer. When I graduated from Mount Carmel Academy, I won a scholarship to Soule Business School. After two years there, I worked in the downtown business world, and then our country entered World War II. Like most girls, wives and mothers, all the women who were left at home worked and prayed and waited for our fighting men to return. In 1944, I married my sweetheart, Herbert Rodrigue, and we lived in an apartment that was built in the basement of the family home on General Haig Street. After a while, we left Lakeview and built our home and raised our two children, Michael and Cheryl. I had a good life and many happy memories of living in Lakeview during the days when it was mostly vacant land. Presently, everything has changed, but it is still an ideal place to live and raise a family.

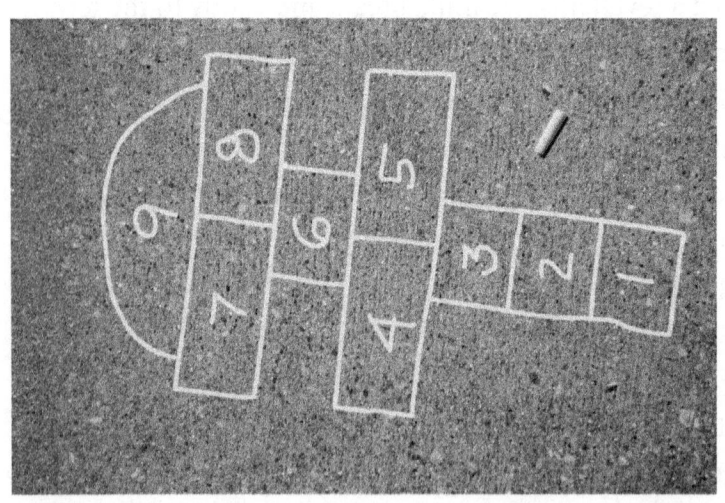

◀ Hopscotch is a game played by children. The pattern is drawn with chalk on the sidewalk or other smooth surface. Players hop on one foot in each square.
Courtesy: Rachel Rivera

ROBERT ROESLER

By the time I was five, both of my parents had died of a terrible illness. It was then that my two sisters and I came to live in Lakeview with my very dear grandparents, Mr. and Mrs. Roesler. They finished raising my two sisters, Lilie and Erna, and me. They lived in a house on Woodlawn Place.

We attended Lakeview School, which by the way is still standing although abandoned. Later we attended Beauregard Grammar School through seventh grade. There was a morning assembly at Lakeview School where we sang, and then Miss Pecoraro played the piano march as we went to class. I can never forget my beautiful kindergarten teacher, Miss Medair. We all loved her. I was not one of the bad ones who got hit on the hands with a large ruler.

I made many friends in my neighborhood. We all played outdoors most of the time. Since I lived close to West End Boulevard, I was near the large green, grassy area between the street and the banks of the New Basin Canal. There was nearly always a group of guys playing ball on the green grass area. Among my buddies, who met nearly every day, were the Connick brothers, Billy, Jimmy and Harry. There was also Dave MacHauer, Jack O'Neil, Harry Philibert and A.J. Negrotto. We considered it our favorite swimming spot like every other kid living near the canal.

There was a heavy bridge called the Black Bridge. When there were no trains scheduled, the bridge was raised high into the air for the barge traffic to get through. A few of us daredevil guys loved to climb to the top and dive into the canal. What a thrill! Of course, my grandmother caught me at this sport, and I really caught it when I got home. As a precaution, I hid a pair of dry pants by the rocks under the bridge.

One day when the bridge was down waiting for a train, I ran across the bridge to test the depth of the water on the Metairie side of the bridge. Soon the train passed, and before I could get back to the bridge, it was raised high into the air. Gosh, that was a long walk along Metairie Cemetery to City Park Avenue past the Half Way House or, as some called it, the Double Dip ice cream parlor. I turned left past the Greenwood Cemetery along the

Street car tracks to get back to my Lakeview home. In those days, we did a lot of walking, skating, and bike riding. There were few cars on the streets.

My grandparents did have one car, however, and took us many times to the beach and amusement park at Spanish Fort. There was a big sandy beach there and a boardwalk with rides and popcorn and hotdog stands. It was a good place for picnics and family entertainment.

In addition to all of the recreation that we had growing up, boys also found small jobs to have pocket money. My first job consisted of taking tickets at the Lakeview Theater on Harrison Avenue where my aunt was the cashier. My Uncle Robert owned the theater. I loved that job because I got to see movies for free. Late at night when the show closed, I then had to put up signs advertising the coming feature attractions on some of the billboards on Canal Boulevard. Walking home was never a problem. Streets were safe and many neighbors would sit on their front porches in the dark to enjoy the night air. They never lit the porch light because it would attract mosquitos and various bugs.

As time went by, I attended Warren Easton High School, and at fifteen, I tried to join the Navy but was turned down because I was too young. I then lied and joined the US Merchant Marines. At sixteen, I finally joined the Navy. After all, there was a war to win, and I had to get into action. At the end of World War II in 1945, I left the service and found a job immediately with the *Times-Picayune* newspaper.

Not too many years later I married an uptown girl, and we started a family of our own. My Uncle, Robert E. Smith, sold me a home very near where I grew up in Lakeview. It is here that I raised my family. My heart is here where so many happy years of my life have passed. The neighborhood has changed and grown, but it is still my favorite place to live.

▲ The Black Bridge, the bridge that spanned The New Basin Canal for trains to cross. The bridge would raise up for sail boats and barges to travel the canal. The small building housed the bridge tender. Courtesy: New Orleans Public Library

Sister Angele Marie Sadlier, O'carm

Written by: Sister Angele Marie Sadlier, O'Carm
Originally, ELMA MARIE WILHELMINA ANGELA SADLIER

To recall Lakeview of the 1930s and 1940s makes me experience both nostalgia and joy, for I cherish those years. We lived on 302 Harney Street after we moved from Miro Street in the summer of 1934 when I was three. It was a small home with three very small bedrooms and a bath on one side and a living room, dining room and kitchen on the other. We were eight packed in: my parents, Angela and Claus Sadlier; and four brothers, Sterling, Ronald, Claus, and Gerald. We were each about two years apart. We also lived with my mother's youngest brother, Willard, whom Mama and Daddy reared until his marriage, and I was two years younger than Gerry, my youngest brother. Best of all we had a small front porch from which we only had to walk across a sidewalk to get to Lakeview School and the front yard of which made a wonderful playground. Along that sidewalk was, and still is, a row of houses all facing the school.

Lakeview School, which we attended, had excellent teachers, and they were all unmarried because there existed a law requiring that public school teachers not marry. When the law was repealed later in the '40s, most of my teachers married. I still recall Miss Coleman telling us in second grade that if we took less than two minutes to brush our teeth, they were not cleaned well. And I still cherish memories of my kindergarten teacher, Miss Spindler, speaking gently with, not scolding, a boy who wet his pants and then taking him to our little rest room to change his clothes. There was Miss Maloney, who bravely had us make butter in third grade and dip bottles into mixed paint to make vases as gifts for our mothers. She also took us to see the plants and flowers at a nursery a couple of blocks away on either Milne or Catina streets. In fourth grade, Miss Gonzalez, a marvelous English teacher, at the risk of losing her job, challenged a boy to behave morally. Miss Lucy Dalier in fifth and sixth grade was my idol. I loved learning in her class. In seventh grade, we had a teacher with poor discipline, who would go get Miss Dalier in the next room, whose very presence brought us to silence, not because we feared her, but because we all loved and respected her. Then since there was no eighth grade, I went to Mount Carmel Academy and graduated after eleventh grade.

In those days, public schools would allow the Catholic children to leave school at

2:20 p.m. in order to walk to St. Dominic School, the old school five blocks away, surrounded by Harrison Avenue, Catina, Milne and French streets. We would walk down Milne Street, and if the small canal was dry, jump back and forth along it. It had water only when it rained well. Sometimes we would go through the large pipes that were under the street at each corner. I recall Miss Betzer, our principal, assembling all of us "public school catechism kids" to scold us because some children had skipped catechism. The Sisters of Mount Carmel and one year the Eucharistic Rural Dominicans obviously kept role call.

All children preparing for Confirmation had to take a test. Ebbie, a St. Dominic student who lived across the street on Catina, was scheduled to be tested at the same time as Lakeview School students. Being proud, and since I was determined to show that a public school student could do as well as one from St. Dominic, I memorized our sixth grade Baltimore Catechism book from cover to cover. We both got a 99 percent. I don't know what she had wrong, but I spelled "blessed," "blessard." The bad part was that we had to sit in the first row of church for Confirmation being presided over by Archbishop Rummel, which frightened me greatly. However, he called on us as a group rather than individuals, and we all knew the usual Baltimore Catechism answers: Who made us? Why? and others.

▲ Anjelle Saterlee as Queen of the May, a former Mount Carmel Academy student. Presently a Carmelite nun and retired teacher. Courtesy: Mt. Carmel Academy

During World War II, Lakeview School had a huge scrap pile for metal to be used for making bombs. The teachers must have had a headache keeping children from playing by it or on it. Also, during the war, each grade at Lakeview School had a portion of the lot on the west side of our home for growing a victory garden.

Perhaps one of my happiest memories at Lakeview School was our annual festival with a special theme for the entertainment. I recall being dressed as a mocking bird one year and as a Russian child another year when each grade danced to one of the melodies from the Nutcracker Suite. We also enjoyed going annually as a class on the street car to take flowers to place by the statue of John McDonogh, who gave generously to establish public schools in New Orleans and Baltimore.

Along one side of our home was Milne Street and a small canal along which a woman would pass with a cow to graze in an empty lot several blocks down. We raised chickens. My aunt on Ada Place raised three cows and chickens. In the area where I-610 passes now, and on the side of what was then the Florida Avenue canal, there were some Italians who had small farms. Regularly, one of the men would come to our home to sell fresh vegetables. The canal led to a pumping station in the area near City Park. Part of Canal Boulevard was a canal also. Very few homes were on the other side of Canal Boulevard between Florida Avenue and the lake, and there we could gather blackberries in the empty lots. We also used nets to catch crawfish in the ditches. By the West End street car line, there was the New Basin Canal in which barges passed as they brought produce toward town. Boys would swim in the canal and grab watermelons off the barges. However, sometimes the men would just throw them to the swimmers. Along the street car line there were shelters extending over the basin for passengers awaiting the seven-cents ride to town or to the end of the line by Robert E. Lee Boulevard. We would also use the shelters for putting down our crab nets, although my parents preferred crab, fish, and shrimp from Lake Pontchartrain, which was cleaner. Frequently, we biked to the lake for swimming.

To this day, when the marsh fire smoke comes our way, I experience nostalgia as I recall enjoying the smell of the smoke from the simmering cypress roots, especially from the area around where Bucktown is today. My only fear was that maybe the burning roots would spread to under our home, which I learned later was quite unlikely because just a few feet down we could find water if we dug deep enough, which one time we did.

In the evening while we would be playing in front of Lakeview School, Dad would sometimes tell us two dreams: The first one was that a mail carrier would come walking down Harney Street and deliver his Navy pension from WWI. Financially, we were

▲ The Mother House at Mt. Carmel Academy. Designed and built by architect William Molano. Work began on the building in June of 1925 and was completed July 16, 1926. The building housed a chapel, living quarters for the sisters, and classrooms. Courtesy: Mt. Carmel Academy

▲ An aerial view of Mt. Carmel Academy, 2000. The photo shows the new school building that was added to the original structure, to the right of the Mother House. Courtesy: Mt. Carmel Academy

struggling because of the depression days following 1929. Two, that one day we would own the old, dilapidated three-story house across the street from us owned at that time by a Mrs. Knight, whom we called the Balloon Lady because she always seemed to have balloons in the second floor back windows. Because sometimes Daddy would say that the winter clouds above looked like snow was going to fall, and it usually didn't happen, we assumed that his dreams would also not be realized. Yet both happened, and when I was eight or nine, we moved into this wonderful dream house on 5855 Catina Street, which in time was renovated. The third floor, which has four wings big enough for four bedrooms, a small dining room, a sink, and a shower, became the domain of my brothers, and for my mother, a blessing!

Our home on 5855 Catina Street became a neighborhood hangout with my brothers' friends and mine. Sterling rigged up a radio station with a mike on the sidewalk through which we could talk to a radio on the third floor. We also had a wireless set through which we could communicate from floor to floor in Morse Code, which Dad, who had been a wireless operator in the Navy during World War I, had taught us. The basement contained Daddy's work bench, a laundry, a picture developing dark room, a stage for plays, a projector room for showing movies that my brothers produced and filmed, and a museum, which contained a twenty-or-so-foot anaconda snake skin and many other biological specimens. Also, in the basement, my brothers built a two-story doll house, which I seldom played in because I preferred to play ball with my brothers and neighbors in our backyard, which extended to Milne canal. A front-screened porch was also downstairs. Later my parents, after most of us had moved out, decided to build living quarters for themselves downstairs. Since my brothers were all in bands in Lakeview School, Warren Easton, the American Legion or jazz bands, our home was always filled with music, symphonic being the favored choice. Sometimes we had concerts for our relatives and friends.

Since during World War II families who had extra rooms were asked to rent rooms to families of soldiers, a mother and two daughters, one my age, moved into the second floor apartment, which we had been using for my bedroom with a living room and an extra bath. With also a kitchen, it was a complete apartment. They shared a sad story. When Pearl Harbor was bombed, Mrs. Silvi's husband quickly ran out of their home to go on duty. Their little boy ran trying to follow him. As she ran and shouted in an attempt to stop him, an airplane machine-gunning soldiers on the ground struck and killed her son as she helplessly witnessed it.

At least one other family moved into the apartment when the Silvi family moved out. Also during the war, we folded bandages at the Presbyterian Church on the corner of Polk and Catina streets. At Mount Carmel, we knitted warm apparel and folded bandages too.

While I attended Mount Carmel Academy, across from us on Robert E. Lee Boulevard was a hospital for servicemen. On Sundays, we would sing during Mass for the patients. Farther down was a prisoner's camp with, as far as I recall, young German captives for whom I felt sad since they didn't look any older than my three brothers and some cousins who were also in the service.

We could see them when they cut grass along Robert E. Lee on the lake side because there were camps for our soldiers and sailors where the University of New Orleans now is.

During the war, on Pontchartrain Beach, amphibian boats used to practice coming ashore, which made deep holes in the sand. I recall while swimming there, I assume after the war, two small children, perhaps three years old, running out into the water and sinking into the holes. I dove in and reached one of them, popped my head above water and called my uncle to come in for the other child, which he did. It surprised me that their mother, instead of hugging them because they hadn't drowned, scolded them for going there.

Pontchartrain Beach also had that fun-packed amusement park where we used to stand and laugh with the enormous laughing lady. City Park also was inviting with its spacious

Mt. Carmel Academy (in background) overlooks "Camps for rent" in this 1926 photo

▲ A view of the fishing camps that line Lake Pontchartrain. Mount Carmel Academy can be seen overlooking these camps in the background. The Mother House faces Robert E. Lee which, at the time was near the shores of the lake. Courtesy: Mt. Carmel Academy

swimming pool and its large, old oak trees with branches for climbing. Unfortunately, when pools needed to be integrated, it was closed for swimming and ironically converted into a monkey island for a while, then closed for good. So sad a commentary on racism.

While we were still living on Harney Street, we experienced another very sad occurrence of racism. It was understood at that time that no colored people, as we called them, were allowed to live in Lakeview, nor were they to be seen in Lakeview after dark. Since my mother and father both needed to work, after school, a young black woman, Julia Normand, would come to watch us until Mama and Daddy would return. She was saving money in order to go to nursing school. On a particular day, because Mama was ill with the flu and Daddy had not yet returned, Julia offered to stay longer to feed us and prepare us for bed. Mama reminded her that it would be dangerous for her to leave after dark, but she commented that it was only a short distance to the street car stop and that she would be safe. Safe she was not. Some men picked her up, beat her brutally, pinned an awful note Daddy wouldn't tell me the words on it—telling her that she and her kind were never to be seen in Lakeview after dark again and then dropped her on the side of a road in a "black" neighborhood. Daddy took us to see her in the hospital. She was so terribly bruised and swollen. I asked Daddy why someone would do something like that to someone so kind as Julia. He responded something to the effect that not everyone realized that we were all God's children. Incidentally, Julia did go on to become a nurse.

Since we could catch fish, crabs, and shrimp in Lake Pontchartrain, we never needed to buy these items when they were in season, which was just about all of the time. For shrimp bait, we would dig up clams in the shallow water in Little Woods, crush them and then throw them into the lake by the seawall, usually around No. 99. In Little Woods, we would also find soft shell crabs seasonally. For fishing, we would use the narrow tip of a bamboo pole to chase out baby crabs from the cracks in the seawall dividers. My uncle, a biologist, insisted that the little crabs didn't feel pain when we hooked them near their flippers before casting them out as bait. Dad also went fishing with his friends, usually a brother-in-law, at camps by the Rigolets or Lake Catherine and sometimes on the Northshore by Slidell.

Along the lake, there was also a drive-in theater. Since funds were not readily available, instead of going in, we would park along the lake and sit on top of our car from where we could not only watch the movie but also usually hear it unless the winds were too strong and blowing south.

Once in a while, we would attend movies at either the Beacon or the Lakeview Theater on Harrison Avenue. During World War II, movies of battles were also shown to keep up our patriotism. And such songs as "Any bonds today, bonds of freedom, that's what I'm selling, any bonds today" would penetrate our beings, and we would take our few nickels and buy stamps to try to fill up our stamp books. Another World War II memory was rationing. To avoid hoarding, if you needed more toothpaste, you needed to bring your empty tube to the drug store, which for us was on the corner of Polk and Milne streets. Also, since sugar was rationed, my mother lined up five cans, large down to small, for us five children. That way it would last us until the next time it could be purchased. Of course, as one of my brothers went into the service, the cans, bit by bit, disappeared.

While the new St. Dominic Church, now the parish hall, was being built and the old church by Catina Street was being used for classrooms, Sunday Mass was celebrated in the Lakeview movie theater. On one Sunday, I noticed that the "coming soon" signs on each side of the screen were advertising the movies *Heaven Can Wait* and *You Can't Take It With You*. Given our Sunday worship each week there, sometimes we would find ourselves genuflecting as we entered our row at the theater for a movie.

My four brothers usually biked to and from Warren Easton. All marched in the band for parades and for ball games. The game between Easton and Jesuit was the only high school game played at Tulane stadium, one of the only games that I attended. I recall being so joyful during a Warren Easton concert when Ronald played the French horn solo, a part of Tchaikovsky's *Fifth Symphony*, and which I found out years later he had made the arrangement for the high school band. Claus and Gerry also played the French horn; Sterling, the trombone. As Claus and Ronald became professional musicians and played in symphonies as well as taught music, they became skilled with most instruments. Claus also had his own "Umpapa" band. Gerry taught music for a while, but then shifted into communications on the college and university level. Except for playing the trombone in the service, Sterling did not continue in the music field.

Some might recall the Pelican baseball team. Daddy sometimes took me to watch them play on Ladies Free night, which I believe was on Thursday. In fact, as my brother Ronald recalled recently, Daddy relished taking us to events and places that were exciting and enjoyable, whether it was to watch the lake rise wildly at the beginning of a storm or to see the results after the storm had passed, to get our Christmas tree, mistletoe, and holly in the Mandeville woods or to get spring water at a spring in Mandeville, to go fishing in Bay St. Louis, or to explore the old fort at Fort Macomb. Mama usually accompanied us on the excursions.

I also witnessed my mother's generous giving. Once when I was three, a lady came to ask for food for her little girl and for a baby on the way. Mama gave her canned food from our own sparse pantry, including canned milk, which I heard Mama say the lady would need with a new baby coming. Then she pulled down our baby clothes and gave them to her knowing that she would need them more than we did at the time. She and Daddy allowed numerous people to stay on our third floor after my brothers and I had left home. I found a box of thank you notes from many people who stayed there and also from people whom they had lent money to and in some instances, had later written off the debt.

In 1947, after graduating from high school, I joined the Congregation of Our Lady of Mount Carmel, our Carmelite congregation with headquarters at 420 Robert E. Lee Boulevard in Lakeview. In 1947, this four-story brick building, which had been built in the 1920s, housed all of Mount Carmel Academy, a two-year teacher's Normal School, the leaders of our congregation, our sisters who taught at the academy and for a while at St. Dominic, student boarders, and the postulants and novices in our three-year formation program. Until the mid-1940s, in the backyard, our sisters raised chickens, a cow, and a bull.

JOSEPHINE CARTAZZO SANTORA

I am proud to say that my grandparents left their home in Italy to go to the United States seeking freedom and a new way of life and not for a handout. There were Gaspar and Camille Meo and they were one of the first families to build a home in Lakeview on Milne Street. For years, my grandfather made a good living selling vegetables from his horse-drawn wagon.

When my parents, Annie Meo and Joseph Cartazzo married, they moved into the half double owned by my grandfather. I was born in Lakeview. I had an older sister, Rosemary, who was in high school at the time. My mother died when I was six. Later, when my father remarried, I stayed living with him and my stepmother, but my Aunt Lena and Rosemary were very close to me. In fact, I spent so much time with them that I feel they loved and raised me through my early years. My Aunt Lena lived in Lakeview with my Uncle Sam at 804-806 French Street.

Every day my sister walked me to Lakeview School, and my Aunt Lena picked me up every afternoon. I attended Lakeview School until I graduated from eighth grade and then attended John McDonogh High School for girls. I had many friends and playmates. I still remember some of them and keep in touch. There was Carol Talutto, Catherine Aloise, and Grace Urrata. I'll never forget our principal, Miss Betzer. She carried a large hand-operated bell, which she used to call us to class every day. She was also noted for her large ruler, which was used on boys who misbehaved. She ran a tight ship in those days. I enjoyed athletics and had a good coach, Mr. Breland. I played baseball and was on the track team. Either at school or in our neighborhood, we played many games like hop scotch, hot potato, dodge ball, and jump rope.

My young days were happy ones either at school or vacation time when we enjoyed trips to the City Park swimming pool. My friends and I did not swim in the New Basin Canal. There were many other attractions for us to enjoy in City Park. We paddled boats in the lagoons, and on Sunday nights there were free concerts on the grand stand. When the band did not play, there was a free movie. We always played outdoors when the weather was good. We fished for minnows in the canals, and how can I forget the small wooden bridges across the canals? I lost balance once and fell into the Milne canal and again in the Harrison Avenue canal. Fortunately, they were not deep, just dirty. Then there was the ice man who delivered his ice to our houses for the ice boxes. No electric refrigerators in those days. When he went into a house to make a delivery, we jumped onto the truck to get a chip of ice to eat and cool ourselves off. He never complained. He just chased us off when he was ready to start for the next delivery. Another place we found to cool off was the air-conditioned picture show on Harrison Avenue. There was also The Beacon and the Lakeview, where we went some nights at the cost of fifteen cents. Then there were times when we rode the street car down Canal Street to shop with mothers for shoes and other things and enjoyed the air-conditioned stores like Maison Blanche and D.H. Holmes. Families cooled their homes with window fans, which pulled the cool breezes from Lake Pontchartrain into the rooms.

There was a big amusement park at the entrance to Bayou St. John, which was called Spanish Fort. There was a small sandy beach, bath house, and boardwalk where there were rides, food, and picnic tables. This was later moved to a beach at the end of Elysian Fields Avenue, which was called Pontchartrain Beach. It was really big and we enjoyed rides like the Zephyr and the Whip and sometimes entertainment like circus high-wire acts. One other fun spot was where the New Basin Canal entered Lake Pontchartrain. This was a favorite spot to drop our nets and catch crabs. There was always enough for a whole meal, crab boil, or gumbo. The street cars went by regularly, and the riders would watch us pull in our nets. Very near the West End lighthouse was a place that sold watermelon by the slice. We loved going there and getting a slice for a quarter and then sunning ourselves for a tan.

When it was time to attend high school, my father drove me to John McDonogh High School because it was on his way to work. Sometimes I met friends at the fruit stand on the corner of Broad Street and Esplanade Avenue near the school. We played the juke-box until it was time for school.

After the end of World War II, I met a boy whom I later married. Gerald Santora was in the US Navy, and when he finished his tour of duty, we were married in 1956. The services were held in the school gym, which was located behind the present-day St. Dominic Church on Harrison Avenue. Our wedding ceremony was the last one held in the gym on a Sunday. The church no longer holds wedding ceremonies on Sundays.

We stayed in Lakeview in our apartment at 5836 Canal Boulevard until the city took over all of the property in that area to build the expressway. We then left Lakeview to make our home in Metairie, where I presently live. We had one baby girl who we named Debbie. She has made her home in Dallas now.

Thinking back on my childhood growing up in Lakeview, I can only recall happy times. We were content with what we had not knowing the hardships most of our parents had trying to survive the country's depression. I would not wish to have lived anywhere else. City houses were built so close together while we had so much space for playing in all of the vacant lots and enjoying the advantages of a suburb. Life here was absolutely ideal.

▲ Paper Dolls were very popular with young girls. Paper Doll, "Dolly Dingle by Grace Drayton" 1922. From Pearlmatic. Courtesy: Flickr.com

ROSEMARY SPIES SCHWARTZ

Written by Rosemary Spies Schwartz

My family lived on Polk Avenue. The canal ran alongside our house and my folks planted a lot of ribbon grass to hide the unpleasant view of the algae growing in the canal. I lived there from 1925 until 1946 until I married and moved to the northeastern part of the United States, where I still reside.

My childhood in Lakeview was great. My friends were all close neighbors. The Peyroux family lived a block down from us. There was Alice, Gloria, Audrey, and Arnaud, all kids who played and went to school with us. There was always someone around to come out and play all types of outdoor games like kick-the-can, hide and seek, a tisket–a tasket, jacks, and others. We also made colored sand to sell to friends for buttons.

The most fun was in the summertime when we went swimming in the New Basin Canal, which was only two blocks away. We had a wharf to dive off, and we loved to show off with our fancy dives when a street car came because we were right next to the car stop. Putting small shells on the tracks was a big deal to hear them crunch.

Many days my mother had my brother, Claude, and we would go crabbing with our nets to drop into the water by the street car station, so that she could make gumbo that same afternoon. Another fun place was along the seawall by Lake Pontchartrain. My father had shrimp nets, which he cast out into the water to catch shrimp. Once he tossed them onto the shore, my brother and I had to sort them out for size so that my mother could fry the large ones and stew the smaller ones.

Sometimes I rode my bike from our house all the way to Canal Boulevard and Navarre Avenue to the Liberty Star Grocery to pick up an order for my mother. We rode our bikes everywhere. At the old St. Dominic School, I joined the CYO and played softball with that group. One very good player was my friend, Catherine Healy.

Other good friends I had in Lakeview were June and Joyce, who lived on Catina Street. I saw them mostly in McMain High School. We rode the West End street car together and made four transfers altogether to get to the uptown school.

Back at our house, my older brother, Ignatius "Iggy" Spies, made a very nice miniature golf course on our side lawn. He was trying to charge an admission fee from his friends, but money was scarce, so I don't think he was too successful with that business.

Another great childhood memory was making our own kites. My father took a hatchet and cut cypress stumps from the lot. He cut a section off with his pocket knife and made sticks one-quarter inch thick and one-and-a-half inch long. It took three sticks to make a kite, and he showed us how to tie them. Then we covered them with tissue paper, which we pasted on. The tail was made from all kinds of strips of rags tied together. We flew them over Mr. Schackais' hot houses on Milne Street near our house. If they broke loose, they went as far as Canal Boulevard, and sometimes farther until they snagged in a tree.

I am so glad to have such happy memories of growing up in a place like Lakeview.

▼ Marbles were very popular with young boys. "Marbles" by Rich Bowen 2008. Rights: Attribution 2.0 Generic (CC BY 2.0) Courtesy: Flickr.com

Robert E. Smith
Story courtesy of Lupo Enterprises

Robert E. Smith was one of the most important real estate men of the 1920s and '30s. According to his grandson, Robert Smith Lupo, Smith worked for the railroad at a very young age before he joined the New Orleans Land Company as a real estate agent and became quite successful. He was a very wise business man even through the Great Depression. He and his wife did not live lavishly. He was one of the earliest builders in Lakeview. He either sold or bought property one at a time. He often built a house himself and sold it and carefully accumulated enough to achieve success. He and his wife, Hedwig Schwartz Smith, worked very hard. He built the first theater in Lakeview, which he and his wife operated. He was also very generous and donated a tract of land on Milne Street with the provision that only a New Orleans Public School could be built on it. If not, then the land would be returned to him. By 1926, Lakeview Public School was completed and the first students attended. Later in 1958, he donated the corner lots at Canal Boulevard and Harrison Avenue for the first Lakeview New Orleans Public Library.

In his lifetime, he and his wife had only one child whom they named Alvena. She was raised by her parents in their Lakeview home. She attended Lakeview School until seventh grade and then traveled by street car uptown to Eleanor McMain High School. After graduation, she attended Tulane University and also worked for her parents as manager of Lakeview Theater. She graduated from Tulane with a business degree and following in her father's footsteps, became a wise business woman.

Like most other girls of her generation, she fell in love. His name was Tommy Lupo, a World War II hero of the US Army Air Corps. He saw

▲ Robert E. Smith with grandson, Robert E Smith Lupo and granddaughter, Norris Smith Lupo Williams Courtesy: Lupo Enterprises

much action in the Pacific Theater, flying his fighter plane and becoming Commodore Thomas J. Lupo by the end of the war. His plane now hangs in the National World War II Museum in New Orleans.

Tommy and Alvena Lupo spent their lives raising two children in Lakeview and continued to manage and build a very successful business under the name Lupo Enterprises. Their son, Robert E. Smith Lupo, and their daughter, Norris Smith Lupo Williams, now continue ownership. Their mother, Alvena, was an extremely active philanthropist and real estate developer until she died in 2009. She supported many local and national causes including the National World War II Museum, City Park, St. Dominic Church, St. Paul's Episcopal Church, Jesuit High School, the Academy of Sacred Heart, and too many more charities to count. When the flood waters devastated Lakeview after Hurricane Katrina, she encouraged her family and other families to remain and rebuild and continue the progress of restoring Lakeview. Her two children now have families of their own living in and loyal to Lakeview.

It is admirable that through the efforts and hard work of this one man, Robert E. Smith, his devoted wife, Hedwig, and their wise daughter, Alvena, who married the extremely good business man, Tommy Lupo, that so much has been accomplished to carry Lakeview from its pioneering days to the desirable, beautiful, and healthy area of New Orleans that it is today.

▲ The Smith/Lupo family. Seated (left to right) Robert E. Smith, Hedwig S. Smith (wife of Robert), Jennie P. Lupo (mother of Thomas) and George Lupo (father of Thomas). Standing: Alvena Smith Lupo (daughter of Robert), Thomas J. Lupo (husband of Alvena).

▲ The first movie theatre in Lakeview was opened by Mr. Robert Smith and his daughter in 1940. The theatre was located at 800 Harrison Ave. Courtesy: Lupo Enterprises

▼ R.E. Smith's portrait hanging in the New Orleans Public Library, Lakeview Branch
Courtesy: Robert E. Smith Library

CLAUDE SPIES

My parents built their house on the corner of Polk Avenue and Milne Street in 1928. The address is 215 Polk Avenue, and it is still there since Hurricane Katrina and is also livable; although, I do not know the present owner. I was the youngest of four children. My siblings were Ignatius, Helen, and Rosemary. There was a canal along Milne with a gravel roadway along the east side of the canal. Our property was on the west side of the canal, so my parents planted lots of tall ribbon grass to hide the view of the unsightly algae-filled water. My dad had his driveway between the house and the tall grass on the bank of the canal. I remember one day he backed his 1934 Studebaker a little too far, and the car slipped into the canal. He had to get help from Mr. Mac, who owned a service station on Canal Boulevard between Homedale Avenue and the railroad tracks. I guess Mr. Mac was pretty used to pulling cars out of the canals in Lakeview.

There were many vacant lots surrounding our house; therefore, my dad, like many others, used the land to plant a few vegetables and raise chickens. At one time, we had about 300 chickens. On Saturdays, I helped my dad sell eggs for ten cents a dozen. Sometimes we had so many eggs that if the housewives did not have the money, he gave them the eggs free. Needless to say, Sunday dinners were always chicken.

When I was about six or seven, my uncle gave me a baby calf, which I tended to until it grew up. Then I brought it over to Tabby's dairy, which was located nearby between Milne, Catina, Germain, and Ringold streets. He had a bull that serviced my cow. Dad built a shed behind our house to keep our cow, and soon I learned to milk her when she was ready. I then sold milk for ten cents a quart.

My first school was Lakeview School, which was on Milne Street only a block away. I began kindergarten there and stayed until third grade. For some unknown reason, I was transferred to St. Dominic School, which was located on the corner of Milne Street and Harrison Avenue. Both of these streets had canals and only one roadway along one side. The canals turned into huge drainage pipes and were covered with grass and trees. We called these "neutral grounds" with paved streets running along each side.

At St. Dominic, the classrooms were on the second floor above the church, which was a lovely brick building facing Harrison Avenue. Other classrooms were in the old gray hall. This was a small single-story wooden building behind the church. Then behind that was a house for our teachers who were all nuns. I am not sure if they were Dominican or Carmelite nuns whose main convent was on Robert E. Lee Boulevard on the corner of Milne Street. All the streets surrounding the church and school were made of shell or gravel. The Harrison canal was large and open and a good place to catch crawfish. This canal ran across Canal Boulevard and ended at the Orleans Street and the Orleans canal.

At St. Dominic School, lunch was not served; therefore, we either walked home for lunch or bought and ate French bread sandwiches for ten cents at Gordon's Grocery. It was a little store facing the school but across Milne canal.

There was a basketball team, which I joined and played on the space between the rectory and the church. The court was made up of river sand and oyster shells. When our team played the team at Sacred Heart on Canal Street, we had to climb to the third floor of the building and play on their beautiful polished wooden floor. We all thought we were getting a nosebleed just to get all the way up to the third floor.

Along West End Boulevard between the road and the bank where the West End street car traveled, there was a large green area where at nearly every corner, there was a gang of boys playing football or baseball. My friends met on the corner of Brooks Street and West End Boulevard. This was our after school and Saturday playground. I am sure many people riding the street cars enjoyed watching us as the cars stopped at each station. These street cars traveled along the bank of the New Basin Canal. They swayed right and left to the point you thought they would jump the track and land right in the canal. This canal was the main artery to Lake Pontchartrain. It was clean and clear. And from the many car stops built along and extending over the water, it was a good place not only to wait for the street car but to swim and drop crab nets to catch the big blue crabs. Often barges loaded with shells, melons, or other produce from the north shore of Lake Pontchartrain traveled this New Basin Canal bringing their loads to the inner city. Since this was our main swimming hole, we called ourselves "Basin Pirates" and swam out to the barges to get a melon or two. I remember the names of two of Jahnke's boats. They were the Fox and the Crozat. One time we hung onto a cypress skiff behind one of the empty barges returning to the Northshore. We enjoyed the free ride, but when they reached the lighthouse by the lake, we had to walk home.

I loved to go out to the Lake Pontchartrain seawall with my dad. He brought a bucket of clams to use as bait, and he would cast his nets into the lake to catch shrimp. He had an eight-foot net, and I had a five-foot net. We spent many nights out there catching the breeze and bringing home the shrimp.

On the west side of the New Basin Canal was Pontchartrain Boulevard. It too was a shell road. There was a nursery owned and operated by the Talen family, and they used to ferry the WPA workers across the canal from the street car side to work on the banks of the canal. My mother gave sandwiches to the men, egg sandwiches of course!

My first job was the delivery of groceries on my bike. When the telephone became popular, people called in to drug stores and grocery stores and had things delivered by bicycle. I worked for Mr. and Mrs. Drufner in their small store on the corner of Catina and Polk streets. Besides delivering, I did many odd jobs around the store. They later opened a variety store right across the street from our house. They were so well known in the neighborhood that many people called them Aunt Marie and Uncle Roger.

Later I worked at the drive-in theater on the corner of Canal Boulevard and Robert E. Lee Boulevard across from the Rockery Inn restaurant. I did various jobs, like handing out flit cans to spray mosquitos, or I could hop on the running board of an incoming car with my flashlight and direct the driver to a spot next to a speaker to park the car. Some couples asked to get parked as far as the back fence. I guess they wanted to smooch.

Growing up in Lakeview kept me happy and busy with my friends and activities, free from violence and crime. People in Lakeview slept with doors unlocked and had screen doors and screen windows to keep out insects and catch the night breeze from the lake. I look back on those times of total peace and freedom.

When I finished the seventh grade at St. Dominic School, I attended Warren Easton High School for four years until graduation. By then, World War II was taking my friends, and we all went our separate ways. By 1945, when we all returned as veterans, Lakeview, as well as every place in the United States, changed completely. Veterans needed housing, and those vacant lots were selling fast and furiously. New construction of houses and businesses sprang up everywhere. Streets were cut through and paved. The New Basin Canal was filled and the good old street car was replaced by a bus. The entire picture changed. The once country-like suburb has become a modern suburb but still a most beautiful and convenient place to live and an important part of the city of New Orleans.

▲ A boy's delivery bike, common for the period. "The Industrial Newsboy" from Workmans Cycles. Courtesy: Worksmans Cycles

SUE SPILSBURY
Written by Sue Spilsbury

My father built our two-story Georgian-style family home at 5801 Vicksburg Street within six months of my birth, and we moved into it in February 1939. One of my very earliest recollections was of standing up in my brown enameled iron crib and looking out of the front window at night, watching my Daddy participate in a blackout mock air raid, which for years I thought was overly dramatic until I learned that German U-boats had, in fact, found their way into the mouth of the Mississippi River. Daddy's equipment was a tin helmet and a fireman's pickaxe, standard issue for local militia. He and a few other neighbors would mill around and then disband. Harold Leibe, who lived at the opposite end of the block, had civil defense meetings in his garage. Once, my parents took me to a mock MASH unit display on the Marconi Avenue side of City Park Stadium where "wounded" soldiers were treated. Mama and Daddy seldom spoke of the war to me but took me to the drive-in theater at Canal Boulevard and Robert E. Lee Boulevard with my blanket and chamber pot where I slept on the back seat of the Dodge sedan while they watched war movies and anti-Hitler newsreels. Then they went to Rockery Inn across the street on the way home. They went to the drive-in so I could stay asleep. I awoke sometimes during those movies. They got a night out of the house and I didn't need a babysitter.

After that, I remember my first pet, a chick, which I loved to death. Then my girl dog, Lassie, a blonde cocker spaniel, had puppies, and my mother tried to explain that Lassie dug her pups up from underneath the ligustrums. That's how you got puppies. I asked her how come cockers didn't accidentally dig up pointers and that ended all discussions about the birds and the bees and the stork forever.

Next, Lakeview School and kindergarten with Mrs. Andrews, the softest, most lavishly loving teacher in the world, who had us reading right away and who played Prokofiev's "Peter and the Wolf" for our naptime, and I memorized every word and note of it. It was our lullaby. Thank you so much, Mrs. Andrews, wherever you are. I love you.

We walked to school and back with our school bags every day of our nine years at

Lakeview School. The Milne canal, which ran out front, was full of tadpoles in the spring, and we all brought jars of them home while walking past open fields of tethered horses, the grass cutters of the 1940s. Every so often I would jump on one of those horses and take a ride. They always had a fit at first but then calmed down. They never bucked, and it never occurred to me that perhaps they weren't broken. Maybe that's where Mama got the manure for our roses. The Riccobonos lived just across the Milne canal from the school and had a palomino named Bruno that snorted and blew snot all over my dress at Rosemary or Joseph's birthday party. My dress was peach sateen, and I was only eight. This was not good.

Later that year Mama was getting "fat" and told me she had a growth, maybe a tumor, and she would have to go see about it. I told her it was a baby in there, and she laughed. I was right. Lynn was born soon after.

Down Kenilworth Street, looking east a few blocks, there was a dairy farm, and in the misty mornings, you could hear the cows calling softly. Once I went to an auction there, and a man had just bought a baby bull calf and was walking it to his truck. I knew the baby was being taken from his mother, and that was horrifically wrong that she would search and call for him. It hurts me still, and I don't drink milk.

The sounds of handsaws and hammers going all day hung in the air as the neighborhood built up. The ones that went up after I was ten were the new neighbors but never as dear to me as those who were little with me: Edie Leibe, who was raised at Vicksburg and Brooks streets across the street; Emile Mistretta, Gay Latimer, and her little sister, Jean; Rowena Bowab, child-mother of a white leghorn named Cluck-Cluck, who rode everywhere on the handlebars of Rowena's blue Schwinn, and her little sister, Betty; the Salaun boys, Richard Scott, Harris Robinson, Freddy Massett, Jimmy Gilbeau, and Skipper—Skipper who? Later on, the Loubat girls, Joel Bowab and Joy Salaun, became neighborhood pals of my sister, Lynn, who was born when I was nine. Cindy Morris was a neighbor too, but to us big girls, those were the kid sister's pack. We had a second Lassie, a black cocker mix, who we tried to mate with Cindy's dog, Checkers, a gorgeous purebred, but there was no chemistry, and Lassie beat him up for trying to get fresh with her. You go, girl! Our other dog was Cookie, a spotted black and white Chihuahua who used to bite Lynn. We always had Bantam chickens, a Mille-fleur and many Cochins, buff and white.

We were a one-car family, so Mama and I walked everywhere, to the Liberty Star Grocery where the butcher had that enormous carved down butcher block, to the Hill Store, where the Rite-Aid is now at Canal Boulevard and Rosemary Place, and of course,

▲ The Crescent Drive-In Theater. Courtesy: Louisiana Digital Library.

to the Caruso's Canal Boulevard grocery where Glenn, the delivery boy, couldn't deliver. She took me to a little green grocery store called the Rosemary Place Grocery, between Homedale and Florida streets. It had screen doors in the front. There was Cerniglia's Pharmacy. A teenage girl, I think named Nancy, worked there. I will never forget how cheery she always was and how sweet she always was to me, just a little girl. Cerniglia's was just before the railroad tracks across the street from Kirsch's Sinclair Oil service station, which was next to Holbrook's Pharmacy on the corner of Canal Boulevard and Homedale Street. Mr. Holbrook, who may have been a pharmacist, was one of Daddy's clients. Does anyone know where the Cerniglia girl is?

We had no air conditioning in the 1940s, so we Lakeview girls spent our lives outside in intensely social groups and rode our bikes together everywhere. We went to the City Park lagoons to try to catch baby turtles, which never worked because our net handles weren't long enough. On Saturdays, I would ride over to Rowena's house with Gay, if my memory serves me yet, and pick her up and others along the way. We rode together to the Saturday afternoon twenty-five cents matinee at the Lakeview Show on Harrison Avenue, and we'd lean our bikes against the west side of the stucco building where they stood untouched until we got out.

If the feature was a horror show, we would flee to the back of the show during the scary parts, the worst of the worst of which was the scene in Peter Lorre's *Beast with Five Fingers* where the amputated hand claws its way along the tabletop, dragging its bloody wrist gore toward the evil Mr. Lorre's throat. But that all balanced out with endless Roy Rogers, Trigger and Bullet, Dale and Buttermilk, programming our values and ethics for a lifetime, teaching us straight shooting, honor, loyalty, and how to lead a trouble-free life.

That was subtle teaching. Not so subtle was Mrs. Henry, our math teacher at Lakeview School, who carried a long blackboard pointer stick to crack us with if we didn't give the right answer to her question. There was a center aisle in the room. So if we were confident, we sat close to it. If not, we sat closer to the side walls out of reach but never so far over that it looked like a confession. Her demand was that we memorize our tables, like it or not, no excuses, period, and we did.

Emma Betzer, our rotund, fearsome, German white-haired principal, lectured us at morning assembly about how to live right, and she was stern about not chewing gum. Maybe that was just for the girls. She also announced that the whole student body should do its business at home before coming to school every morning without fail. Even as a tyke, I knew she was so wrong about that.

Our graduation ceremony was held in 1952 at Delgado Barn. What a great place to have a graduation! I was too giddy to be sad, too inexperienced to comprehend the coming loss of a lifetime of my family of friends.

At a pre-Katrina class of '52 reunion on Sammy Zito's barge-offices on the Mississippi River, Patsy Webster was thrilled, as was I, to learn that someone else had memorized "Peter and the Wolf" during our kindergarten naps in Mrs. Andrew's class. There are probably others.

There are not schoolbags anymore, just backpacks. Rite-Aid stands where Lakeview theater was, and the Whitney post-Katrina trailer stands on the vacant lot where the Beacon used to be. The Chase Bank parking lot across from St. Dominic was the site of Lakeview Drugstore that had a fountain and a colored woman soda jerk who made the best banana splits for thirty-nine cents. I ate them all of the time, and nothing happened. Now, I better not even smell one.

There was a Humphrey's Bakery on Harrison Avenue, maybe on the west side of Canal Boulevard where the sandwich shop is now. There was a drive-in ice cream stand where the Lakeview Harbor and dry cleaners is now. And across the street from that, there was a watermelon stand where a slice cost twenty-five cents. The site was covered in clam shells and lights were strung over park benches from one side of the yard to the other. It was pretty and beckoning at night. There were mosquitos, but no West Nile Virus, but everyone knew someone who had polio and the telltale one thinner leg.

We were into everything all of the time. We were not afraid of animals. We gardened. We did not have allergies. We were into the outdoors, especially mud, creature dander, and pollen clouds. That's what did it, I think.

The culture was not fearful or focused on danger, and we turned out pretty fearless, and sure enough, nothing happened to us. We were brought up to be very practical, though. We fixed things. We did not go out and buy a new plastic one. We could still use Grandpa's stuff and Grandma's recipes. Lakeview people are the best.

Mary Skelly Stumpf

Written by Mrs. Patricia Porter Levy and Family

No story of Lakeview would be complete without this well-known civic leader, Mrs Stumpf. She was born September 11, 1896 in New Orleans and died there on September 11, 1978. She and her husband, Edward, moved into their home at 5707 Catina Street, purchased about 1930, and raised their two daughters, Muriel and Nedra, in Lakeview. She became very much involved in St. Dominic Church and Mount Carmel Academy, which her children and grandchildren attended.

She was active in civic work as an officer in the Fourth Ward Progressive Association in 1932 and officer in the Fourth Ward Woman's Old Regular Democratic organization in 1932 to 1933. In 1936, she was president of the Lakeview Civic Improvement Association.

By 1950, she worked full time for Dracket & Dracket Realtors. She also worked as a clerk for the New Orleans Police Department. One of the last projects Mary was instrumental in was the closing of the New Basin Canal in Lakeview and the paving of West End Boulevard.

Finally, she was a member of the Board of Managers for the Louisiana State Museum. Her name appears on a bronze plaque at the Cabildo in the French Quarter. This was in commemorating the Capital Construction and Improvement Commission under Governor McKeithen in 1970.

Our generation owes a debt of gratitude to the fine lady and leader who worked hard to make Lakeview what it is today.

Mary Skelly Stumpf. Courtesy: Mary Skelly Stumpf's family.

Mary Meek Swanson

In August of 1920, my parents bought their house at 5645 Milne Street and were married in the parlor. Not long after, by the end of the year, my brother, Walter Meek, was born. Then came me in 1924 and later my sister, Maxie. Believe it or not, when my parents bought the house, there was no street built yet. They had to walk from Canal Boulevard along Homedale Street to what was to be Milne Street. The cross streets had not been cut through yet. The 5600 block of Milne Street was right off of Homedale Street and many small businesses began to move in. For example, there was a dairy called Bisack's. We walked there to buy milk, cottage cheese, and other dairy products. I am told that this particular area was called Homedale subdivision long before the full extent of Lakeview was established.

▲ The front view of the Lakeview School, it faced the Milne Canal. It was the first public school in Lakeview. The land the school was located on was donated by the New Orleans Land Co. in 1926. The school held kindergarten through 7th grade. 2006 Photo by Muriel MacHauer. Courtesy: Muriel B. MacHauer family.

▲ Rear view of the Lakeview School showing courtyard and large chimney used to heat the school. The courtyard faces Colbert Street along Harney Street. 2006 Photo by Muriel MacHauer. Courtesy: Muriel B. MacHauer family.

Lakeview School will always live in my memory. It was a place to make friends as well as learn the three R's. I attended Lakeview School from kindergarten through seventh grade. Then, at the ripe old age of eleven or twelve, we rode the West End street car, transferring four times to get to the uptown high school called Eleanor McMain High School for Girls. Always after school, I rode the South Claiborne street car downtown to help my parents, who had a small store and sandwich shop on Carondelet Street.

Our play time or recreational time was mostly spent in our backyard with other kids from the neighborhood. We had strict orders not to leave while our parents were at work downtown. On days when they were home, Mama played with us. We always wanted her on our baseball teams. She was a winner. My dad was not well and could not participate in sports of any kind. My brother, Walter, played football with friends around the area. To mention a few, there were L.J. and James Vigerie and Kenny and Louie Rouello. Walter also played right end for the Warren Easton High School team.

Among other fun activities in Lakeview were visits to the Spanish Fort amusement park. My uncle took us there in his Model T Ford. It shook so much on the gravel road that it was just as much fun as the rides at the beach. There was a small sandy beach at the end of Bayou St. John where it meets the lake. Another uncle of mine operated the kiddie train in City Park. We loved to visit him, however, we only rode his train if we had pocket change of ten cents. There were no favors for relatives.

As World War II approached, Walter joined the US Navy just before graduation. When the time came for the ceremony, I proudly walked across the stage to receive his diploma from Warren Easton High School.

My sister, Maxie, married a veteran named George Jackson Allen from New Jersey. They lived in Lakeview and raised eight children, enjoying the progress of Lakeview and the new Hynes School.

My brother returned from the service and made his home in Oklahoma. I married Claude Swanson and remained in New Orleans in 1944. We raised one girl and lived in the uptown section of New Orleans. Eventually, we returned to West Lakeview and enjoyed many amenities and conveniences of such a beautiful suburb.

After 77 years, I now reside in Murfreesboro, Tennessee. I live near many nieces and nephews. How I miss my old New Orleans and Lakeview homes. If memories can console, I feel blessed having such happy ones growing up in Lakeview.

Lena Bacino Turpin

My parents were probably among the first settlers in Lakeview. They already had their home on Toulouse Street, which is now Marshall Foch Street, when my brother, Frank, was born in 1924. It was the home of Frank and Lena Bacino. In 1926, I was born. There were so many vacant lots around at that time that my father and a few other neighbors in the area cultivated the land and grew vegetables. We always had plenty enough for ourselves, and on Saturdays my father drove his truck to the French Market to sell as much as he could. For some reason, this was not too profitable. Therefore, we moved to the Carrollton area of town where he opened a grocery store, and we lived near the business.

Later, when I was five, we moved to Lakeview and lived on Milne Street while our house was being built on French Street. It was a double house, 804 and 806 French Street. There was only one house between French Street and Germaine, so my father farmed all of the vacant land around our house. We were on the east side of Canal Boulevard, which was the main street down the center of Lakeview.

When I started kindergarten at Lakeview School, we did not ride the school bus because the last stop that the bus picked up children was on the lake side of Harrison Avenue. We lived on the in-town side of Harrison Avenue, so we walked to school. I remember walking with my brother while my mother watched from our front porch until we crossed Canal Boulevard on the little wooden footbridge over the canal.

I made many friends with neighbors' kids that lived nearby. One of my best friends was Catherine Bertucci De Rouen, and my cousin, Rosemary Cartazzo Gennaro, who also lived nearby. We played with our dolls and learned to sew clothes for them by hand. At school, there were always games like jump rope and jacks that the girls played. The boys played their own games with marbles and ball in the courtyard. I also took piano lessons for a while but gave it up. We always stayed busy after school or during the summer vacations with only the radio for entertainment and news. We all waited for our favorite programs like *The Lone Ranger* and *Lux Radio Theater*. My parents took us to City Park

▲ Phillips 930A, a common radio from the 1930, used for entrainment purposes. "L1060877" © 2006 Nite_Owl. Rights: Attribution-ShareAlike 2.0 Generic (CC BY-SA 2.0). Courtesy: Flickr.com

on Sunday nights to enjoy the free concerts by the police band. Several dancing schools brought their students to perform on stage, which was the big concrete structure located in front of the casino, which still stands today. All of this was free entertainment. After all, no one had much money in the '30s.

I never learned to swim; however, my father frequently took us to Lake Pontchartrain. There was a small sandy beach by the West End Lighthouse. Sometimes he drove us to the amusement park by Spanish Fort. I played in the sand and in the clean clear water, but never had any formal swimming lessons. As I grew older and rode my bike, there were always friends to join in rides around Lakeview and City Park. The streets were safe for kids in those days.

I finished Lakeview School after the seventh grade; I rode the public service bus to John McDonogh High School. My brother, Frank, went to S.J. Peters High School along with most of the other friends from our neighborhood. Boys and girls went to separate high schools at that time. During those days, World War II began and most of our boys joined the service right after graduation. My brother joined the US Army. I trained to be a secretary. When the war ended in 1945, I met a sailor, Charles Turpin, and we married in 1946 in the St. Dominic gym. The present church was not built yet. We made our home in the Gentilly area, and my brother, Frank, married and moved into the Mid-City area. My parents lived in the family home on French Street until they died, my mother in 1977 and then my father in 1981.

The home on French Street remained in the family. After a divorce, Frank moved back into the family home until his tragic death when Hurricane Katrina struck in August of 2005. Frank decided to remain in the attic to endure the storm. He was found later having died of heat exhaustion, a truly sad moment in our lives.

After living in Gentilly for a while, we moved to the Marigny area of New Orleans, where our son, Charles Turpin III, was born. Sometime later we moved back into Gentilly, and my husband died in 1965. When my son attended Hynes Elementary School, I moved into Lakeview. He later attended Beauregard Junior High School and then St. Aloysius High School, which is now Brother Martin High School.

Presently, I reside in Metairie and have enjoyed my home here since 1968. My memories of growing up in Lakeview are all happy ones. I feel lucky that my parents chose that area of New Orleans to make their home and raise their family. The Great Depression meant hard times for everyone in those days. As kids, we had no care in the world. We stayed happy, enjoying living in an almost country town.

Richard Villarubia

My name is Richard, but everyone calls me Richie. I was born in the Mid-City area of New Orleans in 1935, and shortly after that my parents moved into Lakeview. We lived at 5861 West End Boulevard. I was the youngest of four sons. First, there was my brother, Harry Charles, then Leo, and Jake. I followed my brothers everywhere and enjoyed all the games and activities with them and with the neighborhood kids. We had the most fun in the summertime. There was always a ball game on the grassy area between West End Boulevard and the street car tracks, which ran on the bank of the New Basin Canal. There were many vacant lots where blackberry bushes grew among the weeds. These were there to be picked for our mothers to make pies or simply served with sugar and cream.

What fun we had swimming in the New Basin Canal! This offered the greatest swimming place a boy could ask for. Needless to say, our whole summer was spent cooling off in there. To make it more attractive, there were barges loaded with watermelons traveling across Lake Pontchartrain to sell in the markets downtown. Boys couldn't resist begging and teasing the attendants to throw us a melon so we could float it to shore, divide it, and enjoy a cool treat.

Then there was the old Black Bridge. This was a heavy bridge with railroad tracks attached so that a train could cross the New Basin. There was an attendant who raised the bridge when a boat needed to pass. Then he lowered the bridge to allow a train to cross the canal. Many times boys climbed to the top when the bridge was up, so they could do a steep dive into the water. I never tried this, but once my brother got caught climbing half way up when the bridge began to lower. He simply hung on until the bridge stopped and then fell into the water.

Along the bank of the canal, there were small wooden shelters jutting out into the water. These were built for people to wait for the street cars, which took them downtown.

ST. DOMINIC'S CHURCH, SCHOOL AND RECTORY
Erected by Father Perretta, O. P., in 1923. First Mass on December 25, 1923

▲ St. Dominic Church and School, built in 1924. The church was located on Harrison Avenue between the Milne Canal and Catina Street. The classrooms were on the second floor of the church. A hall, called "the grey hall," was located behind the church. The white building depicted on the left was the rectory where the priest lived. A small house behind the church on Catina is where the Carmelite nuns lived. The structures were demolished and the land sold in 1944. Photo from Historical Souvenir Aprox 1912-1944 St. Dominic Church. Courtesy: St. Dominic Church

These cars traveled to Canal Street, which was the main shopping center and also where our fathers worked in offices or banks or various businesses. Another use for these shelters was a good place for us to drop crab nets to bring home fresh caught crabs for our mothers to cook. What a carefree life we had even though our country was going through the Great Depression and most of our parents were struggling to make ends meet. Most people were friendly and helped each other, and kids always found games to play even on rainy days. We played card games or board games on front or back porches, all of which were screened because of mosquitos. Some of my friends were Harry Connick, Claude Spies, Dave MacHauer, and Steven Enright.

When school time came, our family of boys attended St. Dominic School where classrooms were built over the church at the corner of Harrison Avenue and Milne Streets, both of which had canals down one side. It did not take long to learn the school rules when I met Mother Gabriel. How could any of us forget Mother Gabriel and her green ruler?

After I graduated from St. Dominic, I attended Jesuit High School and was happy to join the baseball team. Once more, I received a good education and good study and working habits. When it was time for college, I went to Baton Rouge and attended LSU where I graduated with a degree in petroleum engineering. Since I was a member of the ROTC, I then went right into the US Army. While at LSU, I met a very beautiful co-ed from Baton Rouge, who became my sweetheart and my wife. I was first stationed in Virginia, then in Missouri where our twin boys were born. World War II ended, and we returned to New Orleans and made our home in Jefferson Parish, where two more of our children were born. I did not return to Lakeview, the wonderful place of my childhood, but I can truly say that I had a good life and still look back with happy memories of growing up in Lakeview.

PART III
IMAGES OF LAKEVIEW

▲ The memorial on Canal Boulevard for the boys that did not return from WWI and Korea. Photo by Michael Dyer. Courtesy: Muriel B. MacHauer family

- The memorial along Florida Ave, located on the neutral ground. The memorial is near Canal Boulevard near the end of West End Boulevard. Under each crepe myrtle, there is a headstone that has the name of one boy from Lakeview who gave their life for their country during WWII. Additional stones were later added for those killed during the Korean War. The memorials are maintained by members of Post 288 of the American Legion. The members place small flags by each and flowers at the large flag and bronze marker on Canal Boulevard.
- "This avenue of trees is dedicated to the memory of the boys of Lakeview who gave their lives in WWII to make light the master of might to promote peace and good will on Earth." Lakeview Post and AUX. 229 American Legion. Photos by Michael Dyer. Photos Courtesy: Muriel B. MacHauer family

▲ The Milneburg Lighthouse: It was once located on the waters of Lake Pontchartrain at the end of Elysian Fields Avenue. The picture above shows the entrance to the Pontchartrain Amusement Park. Today this location is part of the University of New Orleans. Courtesy: New Orleans Public Library

▲ "The Zephyr" the roller coaster located at Pontchartrain Beach, New Orleans, Photo taken 1953. Courtesy: Tulane University

▶ The Lake Pontchartrain seawall. Courtesy: Tulane University

▼ The original lighthouse located at the entrance of the New Basin Canal at West End. The lighthouse was constructed in 1839 and rebuilt in 1854. Photo taken 1910. Courtesy: Tulane University

▲ Newer photo of the original West End light house. Courtesy: New Orleans Public Library.

▲ View of West End Park with Lake Pontchartrain in the background depicted in postcard c. 1906. Postcard reads "West End Park and Lake Pontrchartrain, New Orleans, LA." Courtesy: Tulane University

▲ The camps that lined the shores of Lake Pontchartrain in the early 1900s. Date of photo unknown. Courtesy: Tulane University

▲ This postcard from 1906 depicts the shell road that ran along the New Basin Canal and in modern Lakeview is now Pontchartrain Boulevard. The road ran through Lakeview to Lake Pontchartrain at West End. The Postcard reads "Shell Road Toll Gate New Orleans, LA."   Courtesy: Tulane University

◀ A schooner on the New Basin Canal passes the iconic Black Bridge. Photograph by Alexander Allison, c. 1905 - 1910. Photo in the public domain. Courtesy: Wikimedia Commons

▲ The "Spanish Villas" of Lakeview. These houses were located on Canal Blvd. near Filmore. The homes were built by Dennis Casey of the New Orleans Land Company. The house on the far right was bought by Judge David and Muriel MacHauer in 1958. From "The New Lakeview" by New Orleans Land Company. Courtesy: Derbes family

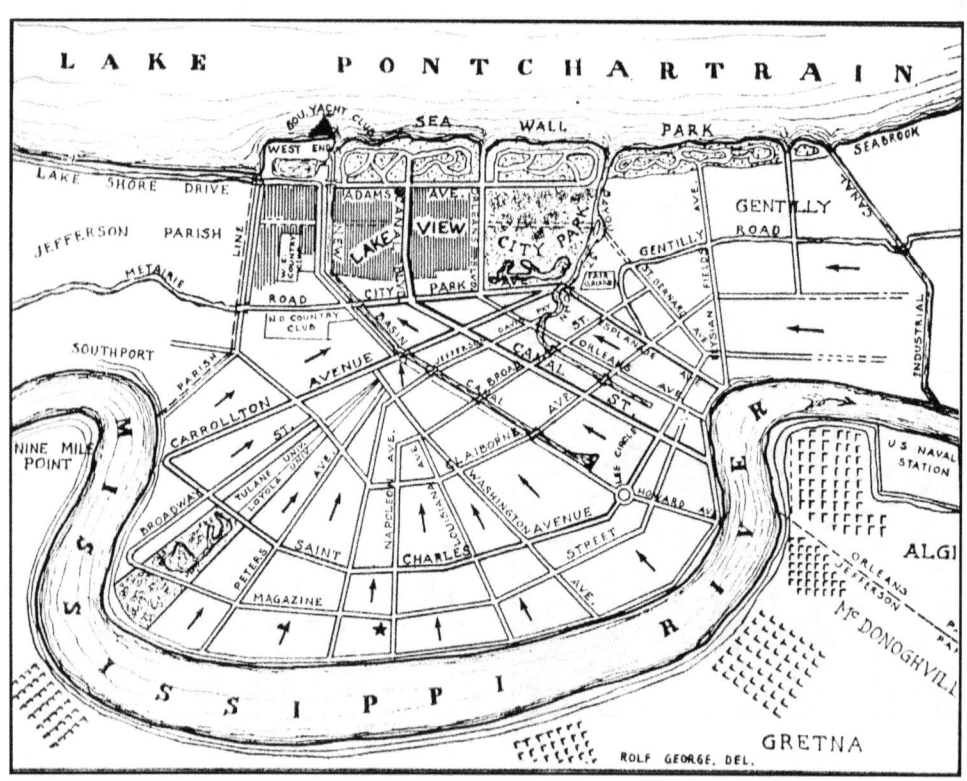

◀ Hand-drawn map of Lakeview. From "The New Lakeview" by New Orleans Land Company. Courtesy: Derbes family

◀ The "House with the Blue Roof" is an iconic Lakeview structure and can still be seen at 6339 West End Blvd. The house is one of the first houses built in Lakeview and was designed by architect H. Jordan McKenzie, built by Robert Markel. The house stayed in the family of Dr. and Mrs. Ernest Celli for many years. During Hurricane Katrina the structure survived, but the lower portion was flooded. The house was restored by the Historic Preservation Society. Courtesy: Muriel B. MacHauer family

▲ The Celtic Cross at the north end of West End Blvd. The cross was placed in the greenspace that was once the New Basin Canal. The cross commemorates the thousands of Irish and German immigrants who came to New Orleans to dig the canal and died of Yellow fever, Cholera and malnutrician during the construction of the canal. The four stones that surround the cross were actually used by workmen. The stones were used to hold the sides of the canal up to prevent the mud from caving in on the workmen as they dug. Courtesy: Muriel B. MacHauer family

▲ The first church in Lakeview. Ave Maria Chapel, located at 209 Chapelle and dedicated in 1912. The church was destroyed three years later in a storm in 1915. Photo in the public domain. Courtesy: Wikimedia Commons

IMAGES OF CITY PARK

- Grand entrance to City Park on City Park Avenue: The entrance is surrounded by many oaks that are hundreds of years old.
- The band stand in City Park: It faces the building called "the casino" and the lagoon. The band stand was used by the New Orleans Police Band, along with many other bands and schools to entertain the crowds on Sunday nights. Photos by Muriel MacHauer. Courtesy: Muriel B. MacHauer family

▲ City Park Swimming Pool. Courtesy: New Orleans Public Library

▲ The oldest structure in City Park, the Peristyle. It was built along the lagoon for dancing and concerts. Courtesy: New Orleans Public Library

▲ The wading pool at City Park, donated to City Park in 1914 by Mrs. Chapman H. Hyams. The pool is still in use today. Photo by Malcolm. MacHauer Courtesy: Muriel B. MacHauer family

▼ "City Park Lagoon Canoe Shade1900" by Photographer unknown - Period photo via WPA collection. Rights: Public Domain. Courtesy: Wikimedia Commons

NEW ORLEANS MUSEUM OF ART

▲ "Delgado Art Museum Dedicated New Orleans 1911" by Staff of the Daily Picayune - Dec. 16, 1911, issue of The Daily Picayune, via Times-Picayune archives. Rights: Public Domain Courtesy: Wikimedia Commons

▲ "Delgado College NOLA 1990s" by Infrogmation of New Orleans - Photograph by Infrogmation (talk). Licensed under CC BY 2.0 Courtesy: Wikimedia Commons

Isaac Delgado (1839 -1912) was a wealthy businessman who was originally from Jamaica. Delgado immigrated to New Orleans with his Aunt and Uncle in 1850. Delgado and his family became very wealthy as sugar brokers. Delgado with no heirs, used his money to improve New Orleans, focusing on the arts, medicine and education.

Delgado used his wealth to fund the first surgical center within Charity Hospital, the Delgado Central Trades School for young boys, which later became Delgado Community College and the New Orleans Museum of Art, which was orginially called the Isaac Delgado Museum.

IMAGES OF SPANISH FORT

◀ The original Spanish Fort: The fort was built by the French and then later improved by the Spanish. It was built at the entrance to Bayou St. John to protect New Orleans. It was used by General Jackson during the War of 1812 and later it was occupied by the Confederate Army during the Civil War. Courtesy: New Orleans Public Library

◀ A submarine built at Spanish Fort: The craft was built during the Civil War and sank in Bayou St. John on its first trial run. It was raised and put on display in front of Touche's Restaurant located at the entrance to Bayou St. John across from the fort. Courtesy: New Orleans Public Library

▲ Spanish Fort, Bayou St. John at Lake Pontchartrain. Photo "Spanish Fort Bayou with Boats New Orleans 1934." Photo is in the public domain. Courtesy: Wikimedia Commons

▲ "Trains approaching station, Spanish Fort, New Orleans, LA" depicted in postcard from 1912. Photo is in the public domain. H. J. Harvey photograph published as postcard by C. B. Mason. Courtesy: Wikimedia Commons

IMAGES OF TOUCHE'S RESORT

▲ Touche's Resort was located across from Spanish Fort at the entrance of Bayou St. John and Lake Pontchartrain. Touche's Resort had a restaurant, bar, dance floor, along with hotel on the second floor and the family residence. Courtesy: New Orleans Public Library

◄ Bayou St. John boating activity in the area by Spanish Fort and Touche's Resort. 1895 Courtesy: Tulane University

LAKEVIEW PRESBYTERIAN CHURCH

◀ In June of 1912, the Mission Committee of the Presbytery purchased the land at the corner of Catina Street and Polk Avenue from the New Orleans Land Co. for $1,000. The Presbyter's Men's Union constructed a one-story building at a cost of $5,000. The second story of the building was added later. It is known as one of the first structures of Lakeview. First Presbyterian Church ,1912-1937, currently Fourth Church of Christ Scientist (1950). Presently standing and serving all members. Courtesy: Mrs. Colleen Moore, active member.

▼ Present building (2014) Church of Christian Scientist. In 1950, the Fourth Church of Christian Scientist purchased the building for $12,000. After many renovations, the building was placed on the National Register of Historic Places, July 19, 2002. Courtesy: Fourth Church of Christian Scientist

THE PORTEOUS STREET HAUNTED HOUSE

▲ The "Haunted" Orchard house at 214 Porteous Street on the corner of Milne. Little is known about the family who built and lived in this house. My only memory is of the 3 children who were driven to Lakeview School each day by the father in a very old antique car. They did not speak or make friends with anyone. Over the years the father and each daughter died in the house and during that time it was neglected and finally abandoned where it sat and became a Lakeview "urban legend." Neighborhood children ran around the house on Halloween pelting it with rocks and vandalizing it. Lakeview residents still talk about the haunted house and wonder what became of the ghosts of the house after Katrina. Photo by Sharon McDonald Palmisano. Courtesy: Homer McDonald

CONCLUSION

In conclusion, I wish to say that this book began as a collection of stories from friends that I found returning after Hurricane Katrina. It is not about that flood and a great disaster. It is about the children whose parents came to build, live, and raise us, their children, in this new subdivision so near Lake Pontchartrain. To me, it began as a hobby, writing the memories of my friends from the neighborhood or from the two first schools, Lakeview or St. Dominic.

We laughed thinking about the good times we had at the beach or at City Park or even in school where strict teachers walked around the room with a yard stick in hand to give a hard tap on hands of bad boys.

The simple things in our lives were so important to us at that time like the ride on the streetcar to go downtown to buy shoes or just to enjoy the air conditioning in the department stores and theatres. Then in wintertime it was a special treat to go to Canal Street to see the Christmas decorations and Mr. Bingle at Maison Blanche and the display of trains and dolls in the show windows of D.H. Holmes. There was no such term as "casual dress". Everyone dressed according to the occasion. Our dads wore straw hats to work in summertime and felt hats in winter. Men who had outdoor jobs wore hats of the trade. Going to church on Sunday, we wore our Sunday dress and hat, not as big and pretty as our mothers, but pretty to us. Boys also wore clean pressed clothes to church. Men always removed their hats when entering a church or building or elevators.

The present generation find it hard to understand so many things that were routine to us. When we were old enough to go on dates, which were usually house parties, we either walked or road the streetcar. Then, when World War II began in 1940, our boys left to join the service to save America. We wrote letters daily, which present day kids cannot believe. How can you write love letters on V-mail? In this day of instant communication, V-mail is unheard of.

At any post office, we asked for a sheet for V-mail. V-mail One sheet for one letter on a special form, to be folded a certain way into a small size and they were mailed overseas. Needless to say how much these letters were cherished by our boys. Finally, this is simply a story of one tiny spot in this world, in this City of New Orleans, in this neighborhood called Lakeview. This is where we grew as happy children while our parents endured our country's Great Depression and the many floods and hurricanes of this area. Lakeview continued to grow and change as we grew and survived, but our memories remain forever and I have endeavored to describe the way it was.

Acknowledgements

My heartfelt gratitude goes to all who helped me in my effort to gather and tell this story of kids lucky enough to be born in this country, in this southern city of New Orleans, and in this new neighborhood during the 1920s and 1930s. In spite of the worries and problems that our parents experienced during those years, we lived carefree childhood days. We knew money was scarce, but we stayed busy with our games both indoors and outdoors and our perfect playground of a neighborhood.

First, I must thank my whole family for patiently listening and recording via modern technology all the memories that I tried to gather in words and pictures. My first daughter Bonnie was my first editor. My son Malcolm, his wife, Brittany, my second son Vernon, and my youngest daughter, Cheryl, contributed countless hours and tasks to bring this to conclusion. I also would like to thank my grandchildren, who gave much of their talent to help me in this endeavor, Jennifer Dyer who provided pictures, Daniel Dyer, and Michael Dyer who helped gather and snap pictures and Rachel Muller Rivera, who designed the cover and put together the interior of the book. I also want to thank my grandson Wesley Muller for editing the book and my granddaughter Mindi MacHauer for her security provided. Thomas Dyer for his constant prayers and support for this endeavor. To my grandson Capt. Dennis Muller, USAF for serving our great country, his service gives me inspiration.

Many thanks to my brothers Walter, Merlin, and his wife Jackie, friends, Mickey Steubben, Rita Palotta, Sisters Therese and Sister Germaine from the Mount Carmel archives and Sister Angele Marie Sadlier O'Carm, Mrs. Yvonne Spear Perret, Mrs. Andree Maduell, Mr James Guilbeau, The Lakeview Civic Improvement Association, Mrs. Colleen Moore of Fourth Church of Christian Science, Mrs. Irene Wainwright of the New Orleans Public Library, Historic New Orleans Collection, Cheryl Ledet, Joan Porter, and John Guidry, and all the individuals who shared their memories to make this book possible.

Thanks a million.

Yours Truly,

Muriel Bonie MacHauer

CREDITS

General Credit Notice About Images & Photography:
Many photographs and images in this publication have been cropped, resized, and enhanced via grayscale and coloring by Rachel Rivera with permission from materials provided by the cited sources.

INTRODUCTION CREDITS

"For Sale." Original advertisements of land to be sold by The New Orleans Land Company. 1925. Courtesy: Historical *Times-Picayune*

"Lakeview Map." Lots planned in Lakeview area of New Orleans from Gardner's City Directory of 1867. Photo in the public domain. Courtesy: Tulane University.

COVER CREDITS

"Girls on roller skates under the palms of the City Park." Uncredited Farm Security Administration/Works Progress Administration photographer. Courtesy: Wikipedia Commons

"Black Bridge" over New Basin Canal in raised position. Photo in the public domain. Courtesy: Wikipedia Commons

Steamer on New Basin Canal - "Exchange Outing Day." Photo by E. J. Bellocq printed in Moyston, Roy C. Architectural Art and Its Allies 4:2 1910. Photo in the public domain. Courtesy: Wikipedia Commons

"Children at playground in City Park, 1939." Uncredited WPA photographer. Courtesy: Wikipedia Commons

www.ingramcontent.com/pod-product-compliance
Lightning Source LLC
LaVergne TN
LVHW061215060426
835507LV00016B/1935